THE WATER RABBIT

Lost at sea ... and finding myself

Carolyn Lee

The Water Rabbit

By Carolyn Lee

ISBN-13: 978-988-8769-34-6

© 2022 Carolyn Lee

BIOGRAPHY & AUTOBIOGRAPHY

EB159

All rights reserved. No part of this book may be reproduced in material form, by any means, whether graphic, electronic, mechanical or other, including photocopying or information storage, in whole or in part. May not be used to prepare other publications without written permission from the publisher except in the case of brief quotations embodied in critical articles or reviews. For information contact info@earnshawbooks.com

Published by Earnshaw Books Ltd. (Hong Kong)

*Dedicated to Captain Sirpreet Singh Kahlon
and all the crew of the* **Maersk Princess**,
31 December 2007

Contents

INTRODUCTION — 1

Chapter 1 – Setting Sail — 5
Chapter 2 – Watching Airplanes — 18
Chapter 3 – Christmas in the Philippines — 31
Chapter 4 – Raymond — 43
Chapter 5 – Out of the Darkness — 55
Chapter 6 – A New Life — 63
Chapter 7 – Pan Pan — 77
Chapter 8 – Dad — 86
Chapter 9 — The Rescue Begins — 101
Chapter 10 – Lost — 107
Chapter 11 – In the Sea — 117
Chapter 12 – May Day — 126
Chapter 13 – I'll Not See You Today — 133
Chapter 14 – Decompression Chamber — 141
Chapter 15 – Everything's a Mess — 151
Chapter 16 — Martin — 163
Chapter 17 – Alone — 173
Chapter 18 – The Water Rabbit — 187
Chapter 19 – By Your Side — 196
Chapter 20 – The Mothership — 207

EPILOGUE — 217

Introduction

The accident wasn't totally unexpected. I always felt something was going to happen. I wasn't sure what and it is easy to look back now and say that, but I did have a sense of foreboding. At the time you put it down to anxiety, to the sense you are undertaking a grand adventure and no adventure comes without risk. This was our big test, after all — could we cross oceans on the yacht? We had done lots of racing and sailing until this point, but if this trip was a success we would take it to the next level with a plan to sail around the world. This was to be mine and Raymond's jumping off point, the start of it all.

Yet, somewhere inside, I knew. I had that sense, lodged deep within me, that it was all destined to happen. There have been elements of my life that have felt that way - mapped out - and occasionally, I glimpsed little signs before they happened. I couldn't change my future, but there were times I was allowed to see a little way ahead. Or, more accurately, to hear. From the youngest age, these voices came to me out of nowhere. I never knew who they were but perhaps this foreknowledge gave me a chance to prepare, to be ready for whatever I would have to face. These could be difficult situations, but not impossible. Not insurmountable. And having some forewarning, however small and ill-formed, gave me the breathing space to allow me to get ready, a chance to gather my wits and quell my fears without the situation overwhelming me completely.

I don't know what you might call it — a spirit guide, guardian angel or intuition - your interpretation would probably depend on your cultural belief system, but I cannot deny the clairaudience I have. It's a male voice and it speaks to me very clearly, without any accent, as clearly and as real as if we are sitting talking to one another right now. And when he speaks it is calmly and without emotion, telling me what is going to happen, so that I can decide how I'm going to handle it. I can't alter it, but I can be prepared for it.

The irony is that I spent some of my childhood practically deaf from frequent ear infections and perforated eardrums. Or maybe it was because I was deaf that I was tuning into something else, some other plane of reality ordinarily out of reach. Who knows? I don't pretend to have any answers here. I have no overarching worldview to explain what appears to defy explanation. All I can give you is my truth and leave it up to you to decide the interpretation.

So, when I found myself in the water, lost at sea, desperately trying to keep my head above the surface, it wasn't totally unexpected. I knew something was going to happen. Perhaps nothing as serious or as perilous as this, and certainly I could never have foreseen how each moment unravelled, pushing me further and further away from the safety and security of everything that sustained life. But the situation wasn't a shock to the system. My mind and body were prepared. And in those final few moments, when I felt as if I could not hang on any longer, when I was ready to surrender to the warm embrace of the sea, that's when one final voice gave me the strength to keep going. Then I knew that this was something I had to go through to come out the other side. After that, it was up to me what path I took.

When I finally came up for air – coughing, spluttering, vomiting into the churning, swirling sea around me — everything had changed. In those few seconds between life and death, I had experienced a monumental shift, and nothing would ever be the same again. I didn't know it at the time. How could I? I was entangled in the drama of the disaster. It was shocking to acknowledge how close I had come to losing my life. But then slowly, gradually, it dawned on me that this was only the beginning. When I had broken the surface there was a death of sorts, only it wasn't obvious at the time. It was only later as I started to make sense of what I had been through that I realised I faced an enormous and daunting task. My way ahead was far from clear. The big question was: where do I start?

THE WATER RABBIT

1

SETTING SAIL

19 December 2007 – Aberdeen Marina, Hong Kong

IT WAS A LITTLE after midday when we finally set off. I made one last dash to the Marine Department in the morning with all our passports to get Port Clearance before our yacht could leave Hong Kong waters. Then I returned to Aberdeen Marina to meet the rest of our crew on board our boat *Purple X*.

There were eight of us for the trip – my eldest daughter Hannah, 20, who was back from Durham University for the Christmas holidays, my son Aaron, 18, also back home from University in London and youngest son Joe, 16, now in his penultimate year of High School. Then there was me, my husband Raymond, his work colleague Lars, our friend and fellow sailor Paul and my new friend Martin who I'd met just a few months earlier. Everyone was very excited, including me, though I felt a little anxious too, embarking on such a long journey across open sea. But we were well-prepared and ready for the adventure ahead.

We'd watched the weather carefully for the last few days and could see that besides a little choppiness coming out of Hong Kong, we were heading towards better weather in the Philippines. I went below for the few final checks and when I was confident we had everything onboard and stowed safely out of the way, I returned to the cockpit on deck. Raymond gave a very thorough safety briefing to the crew then we looked at one another. 'Okay, we're all set,' I said. 'Let's go!'

The sky was sunny and clear as we slipped the lines from the pontoon and motored *Purple X* out of the typhoon shelter. Once clear of the typhoon shelter walls, we raised our sails, something we had done hundreds of times before, only this time we would be venturing much further than the usual cruising areas around the outlying islands, just across the shipping lanes. These were some of the busiest shipping lanes in the world; large vessels ploughed up and down the fairways in and out of Hong Kong, day and night, all year round. And so far, it was all very familiar. As we ventured beyond the Kwo Chau Islands in the easternmost waters of Hong Kong, the realisation started to sink in. We were on our way! Now 588 nautical miles lay between us and our destination of Subic Bay in the Philippines, a voyage that would take around five days on the open ocean.

Soon, the weather clouded over and as the light faded, the temperature dropped a few degrees and we donned our sailing jackets. There was a steady wind of 23 knots so we were making good speed of about five to seven knots, but the sea was choppy and the ride less than smooth. Before long we were clear of Hong Kong waters. It may not have seemed a big deal to anyone else but to us, this was momentous; we had never sailed our yacht this far from home.

We had ordered our 49-foot Oyster yacht back in 2000 after taking some family sailing holidays; we had crossed the English Channel, sailed around the Hauraki Gulf in New Zealand and chartered a yacht in the Whitsunday Islands off the Queensland coast in Australia. On these trips, we'd always had a skipper with us but were keen to learn the ropes ourselves, getting involved and asking lots of questions. They had been fun holidays so when Raymond suggested we buy our own boat I thought it was a good idea. Our children would learn to sail while they were young and Hong Kong was the ideal place to teach them. The tides here are small, only around two metres, and it's warm most of the year which means you can sail year round. Hong Kong has inexpensive public ferries between various outlying islands, so being on the water is commonplace. And since 2005, we had even lived on a 5-bedroom custom built houseboat.

The yacht took two years to build and cost £1 million over the course of its construction. It was an eye-watering figure but since we'd moved to Hong Kong in 1994 Raymond had worked his way to the top of the investment banking tree, for which he was amply rewarded, and now we were lucky to live a very privileged lifestyle, one I could never have imagined for myself as a child, growing up in straitened circumstances. We named her *Purple X* because we loved the colour purple – her giant asymmetric sail was purple – and since we were still relatively new to the sailing world, we considered ourselves 'perplexed' by it all. So for *Purple X* read 'perplexed'.

However, in order to be somewhat less perplexed, and in the run-up to her delivery in 2002, we prepared ourselves by taking our Yachtmasters Offshore certificate to learn how to navigate and read the weather. I also learned to dinghy sail along with our children and we all became qualified assistant instructors. Alongside this Raymond and I took the theory exam to gain a Hong Kong pleasure vessel licence. The license was vital as we couldn't take out insurance, register or licence our vessel without it. The theory exam covered shipping lanes and speed limits and I learned all the legal requirements of taking our yacht out on the sea.

Our yacht was finished at the Oyster boatyard in Ipswich and we held a launch ceremony there in the spring of 2002.

She was beautiful.

THE WATER RABBIT

True quality craftsmanship. Outside she was all white with teak decking and below she had a cherry wood interior, deep blue sofa covers and white curtains over the portholes. She was clean, classy and truly stunning. I stood on deck, looking over this sleek and elegant boat in wonder. Was she really mine? Never in my wildest dreams had I ever imagined owning a yacht, let alone such an immaculately, handcrafted vessel. And yet here we were. It was remarkable to me how far I had come from those difficult days of my childhood when every penny mattered so much. A boat owner! The prospect was both exciting and daunting at the same time. I knew that to do her justice, she would need to be sailed a lot and venture far. But first things first. We had to get to know her and learn to sail her properly. Like proud parents of a new-born we were exhilarated yet also overwhelmed at the task ahead.

I smashed a bottle of champagne across her bow and said the traditional, ceremonial words: 'I name this yacht *Purple X*. God bless her and all who sail in her!' We cheered and toasted with more champagne. Then we took her for a gentle sail out of the marina and up the River Orwell, where she handled beautifully. Afterwards, she was shipped to Hong Kong on the deck of a container ship and her mast and rigging were reassembled by one of Oyster's employees named Barney.

After the delivery, Barney spent an extra week with me and Raymond, taking us out every day, sailing for several hours, literally showing us the ropes! We anchored, tacked, gybed, cooked, climbed the mast, tried various sails and even went for a weekend sail with all the children. Then after he left, we took her out as much as possible. During the week, she was tucked up in her berth at the Aberdeen Marina Club, which was where our houseboat was also moored. But at weekends we were out on the water, practicing our skills, cruising around the islands, sailing into the neighbouring bays, anchoring overnight, getting off to explore beaches and islands and then returning to the yacht at night. We also joined the Royal Hong Kong Yacht Club, which held local regattas and social activities throughout the year, and took racing trips to Macau and around Hong Kong island.

The more time we spent onboard, the more experienced we became. We quickly discovered that at 23 tonnes our vessel was a very heavy machine which could do a lot of damage in the wrong circumstances. The electric winches we'd had fitted for hoisting, trimming and furling the sails, for example, were a particular liability. If you were not paying close attention to the sails, you could end up just grinding away until something broke. I'd started out with fairly romantic notions of yacht ownership and certainly there was something quite special about being aboard our boat when the weather was good and all the crew knew what they were doing. But taking responsibility for such a large vessel and all the guests onboard could be extremely stressful. Of the two of us, I was always the more cautious sailor, my hand poised over the engine ignition frightened the wind might die as we crossed the shipping lanes with a container ship bearing down on us.

'Stop panicking!' Raymond chastised when he spotted my hand. But I couldn't help it. I was often anxious, especially if the children or their friends were on board. Large ships in shipping lanes have the right of way over pleasure vessels and the reason is obvious – they are so bloody big! They can take half an hour to turn around and several miles to come to a stop. I'd stare at those massive container ships heading towards us, fearful of their size, worrying that they wouldn't be able to stop in time before ploughing into us. I'd heard terrible stories of yachts like ours being 'collected up' on the bows of large ships that lay in their path. Huge moving masses that seem far away one moment and meters away the next. That was the reason you needed to leave a decent space between yourself and anything at sea that might destroy you, be it a ship or a land mass. You needed time to manoeuvre, accounting for all the other factors like the weather and sea conditions. Very different to turning car on a road since you could be pretty certain of which way the car would move.

Taking out novice sailors made things even harder. We had to sail the yacht, entertain our guests and ensure everyone was safe with very little help. For me, the most relaxing and enjoyable times on board were in the company of other competent sailors, such as friends from the yacht club. The days, when those on board had at least as much experience as me, I could relax and have fun. There is the old saying: 'There are old sailors and there are bold sailors, but no old, bold sailors.' I wanted to be an old sailor. Even so, there were plenty of hairy moments. We broke equipment, dragged the anchor, tangled our asymmetric sail, got caught in squalls and even sailed through black rainstorms. These are storms where the rain is exceptionally heavy, exceeding 70 millimetres in an hour. On land, a black rainstorm leads to difficult traffic conditions and flooding. Out at sea, a black rainstorm severely impairs visibility. The amount of water falling from the sky is truly incredible. Standing at the helm with water pouring into your face, not being able to see past the cockpit, let alone beyond the bow of the yacht, is a real challenge.

Onboard, Raymond was our Skipper, though the boat was in my name so I was tasked with all its maintenance and ensuring all our documents were up to date. On the yacht, we worked as a team, looking to one another for affirmation and agreement, especially in difficult weather. We learned something new each time we went out and no two days were the same in terms of weather or crew. The thing was, we didn't want to be just 'okay' sailors, we wanted to be good and competent sailors. We tried all sorts of things, some with more success than others. But ultimately, we wanted to keep learning, no matter how stressful it got. That was what I found so engaging about learning to sail. It disrupted our normal routine and gave us opportunities to upskill.

Now we were about to cross the South China Sea for the first time on our own vessel. It was the first step towards our 'Big Adventure'. For some time now Raymond had spoken about his dream of sailing round the world. With this in mind, we had a bigger boat on order — an Oyster 62-footer – due to be delivered in 2009. For myself, I wasn't sure. I knew that I enjoyed day sailing and when we had the right crew, it could be fun. But I just didn't know if I was up for circumnavigating the globe. For one thing, I was in the middle of a degree at Hong Kong University and wasn't due to complete my studies until 2010. Also, I wasn't confident about handling a larger yacht by ourselves.

During a lengthy conversation with Oyster, it became clear that what we needed for this grand adventure was a couple of professional crew. This would give us the flexibility to allow Raymond to take the yacht across oceans without me, then I could fly in to join them once they were in port. I could also continue my studies while enjoying the best parts of life aboard our yacht. After reading so many sailing and yachting adventure stories, a full-time life onboard our yacht certainly seemed very enticing, but I wasn't ready to commit to such a mammoth undertaking. Not quite yet. At the very least we had to find out what it was like to cross oceans on our own.

So in the run up to Christmas 2007, when we were discussing holiday plans with the kids, Raymond came up with the idea of sailing across to the Philippines and back — a distance of around 588 nautical miles each way. He had already sailed across the South China Sea to the Philippines on someone else's boat,

THE WATER RABBIT

now here was a chance to do it ourselves. Everyone agreed the trip was a good idea so we began preparation. I'd discovered, through hard experience, things go wrong onboard when you don't know what you're doing. Getting caught in a squall or breaking something on the boat and having no clue how to fix it made for some pretty anxiety-inducing moments. The better prepared we were the more in control I would feel.

Raymond and I took a Safety at Sea Survival course, a two-day course at the yacht club, to learn what to do in extreme circumstances. We were thrown into an outdoor swimming pool in February, fully dressed in our foul weather gear. Fire hoses turned on us simulated a storm. We were tasked to climb into a life raft at chin level in the pool. We expected to tread water for longer than I thought imaginable. We learned how to link arms to stay above water in the event we found ourselves in the open ocean. It was no fun. At the end of it I felt a more prepared. I also took an Advanced First Aid course for trauma injuries. If something goes wrong 400 miles offshore you can't just call an ambulance. I learned how to stitch people up, how to set compound fractures and how to do an emergency tracheotomy.

Similarly, we needed to know how to fix our boat in a multitude of different scenarios. What would we do if our engine failed or if we lost part of our rigging? We had to be prepared for every eventuality, so we took an Engineers' Course to figure out the common issues of a diesel engine going down. I also took a Radio Operators course offered at the yacht club to ensure I knew how to call for help if we got into trouble and how to use the emergency listening channel on the radio. Finally, in the run up to the trip, we stepped up a lot of emergency equipment on the yacht, installing a satellite phone, in addition to our Marine VHF radio. We updated our flare box with both rocket flares – the type you send up in the air to light up a large area – and handheld flares which you hold and wave from the deck. We also invested in EPIRBS: Emergency Positioning Indication Relocation Beacons. These devices, worn around the neck, would be triggered if we fell into the sea, sending a GPS location to the emergency services. And we added a life raft, a must for anyone venturing offshore.

All our equipment was provided by our sailing friend, Simon Boyde. He and his wife Louise ran a marine supply shop and as experienced sailors themselves, were perfectly placed to give the best advice of what we would require. One Saturday morning in November, Raymond and I found ourselves comparing the relative merits of different bolt cutters. These would be necessary to cut away the rigging in case we got into any difficulty with our mast or sails.

'Hmmm....' Raymond weighed a pair of hydraulic cutters in his hands. 'Well, these hydraulic ones are quite a bit more money but they are good, aren't they? It will be like a knife through butter if we have to cut anything loose.'

I looked at the prices. He was right; the hydraulic ones were much more expensive than the ordinary steel ones – twice the price, in fact.

'Well, let's get the really good ones,' I insisted. 'They'll never go out of date and we can always take them to the new yacht.'

On the day of our departure, Simon came to visit us on *Purple X* to make sure all the safety equipment was delivered, in place and to wish us safe passage. Strangely enough, Joe asked Simon if there was a problem on deck, should we shout 'All hands on deck"?

Simon replied, "Yes Joe, that's exactly what you shout."

I thought it was a strange thing to ask and hoped we would never need to use the phrase.

Finally, before we left, I submitted our 'passage plan' to the yacht club. This was our expected journey plan which was, again, an important and responsible safety measure. In the same way that hikers are expected give the information of their route and departure and arrival times to a third party, we gave the yacht club all the main details of our trip; when we were leaving, our intended destination and how long we expected the trip to take, which was around four or five days, depending on the weather. If we got into trouble at least the yacht club knew where to start looking.

I felt confident, as we sailed out of Hong Kong, past towering skyscrapers of luxury apartments towards the open ocean, that we had done everything possible to make this a safe trip, even to the point of choosing good hands on deck. We recruited three able bodied people. Our friend Paul who had crossed the South China Sea more than thirty times, Lars who was also an experienced sailor and though Martin who had only sailed a handful of times, we'd taken him out on our boat, had seemed very teachable and keen. Plus, as a member of a special operations unit in the British army, he was capable to deal with any crisis and medical emergency.

'Right, who's on watch first?' Raymond called out from the helm.

We had created a watch system to ensure there were always three people on deck at any time over the whole five days. Each watch lasted four hours and for the rest of the time the other five crew members were free to rest in the cabins, go up on deck or help prepare the next meal. The system was crucial to ensure everyone knew what they were doing and there were always three people responsible for sailing the boat, trimming the sails, keeping watch for any ships, checking the weather and ensuring we stayed on course. Though we had programmed the course into the navigation system and were heading in the same direction on the compass bearing south to southeast, we couldn't always go in a direct line. We were under wind power, so small adjustments were needed all the time to stay on course.

I went below to check the food I had brought for our trip. We were on holiday over Christmas and New Year so I wanted to ensure we had decent food, buying good cuts of ham, decent sourdough bread, high quality bacon, eggs, fancy biscuits and cheese, as well as home-made pies and cakes. We even had a couple of Marks & Spencer Christmas puddings which Martin had brought back from the UK. Stored away we also had a few nice bottles of *plonk* for when we arrived in the Philippines. For now, though, everyone would remain sober. There was an agreed 'no drinking' policy aboard while we were at sea. We had to have our wits about us.

About 100 nautical miles from Hong Kong lay a string of oil platforms. I knew it was out there because I was aware that it was sometimes used as a marker in offshore races but I'd never seen it up close for myself. Now I was itching to see the gas flare at the top of the rig – a major milestone on our voyage — but by the time I'd prepared dinner, cleared up and gone on deck that first evening, the rig was long behind us. I was a little disappointed but generally, this was good news. We were making great progress and the more miles we had under the keel, the more everything settled on the boat.

Once we were out of Hong Kong and on the open seas, the weather turned poor and the going was a little rough. The wind was mostly behind us so we put up our big sail which powered us along quite nicely, but there was no question it was still pretty bumpy. Miraculously, I didn't get seasick but I found Hannah on deck looking green around the gills.

'Oh dear,' I said, noting her hangdog expression. 'The weather's going to get better. I promise. This is just the first day or so.'

Hannah nodded, barely able to speak and I wondered, as I went up for my watch from 8pm till midnight, whether she would make it. Five minutes later she staggered into the cockpit to do her bit. *Bless her, she looks wretched,* I thought, but I was pleased she was here.

Despite their privileged upbringing, my kids were not spoiled. I had made sure of that. They were capable, self-reliant individuals and I was proud that Hannah hadn't shirked her duties because of seasickness. Besides, it wasn't long before we left the rough weather behind and after 48 hours we were into 'blue water sailing'. The weather was warmer, the sea calmer and we all changed out of our long trousers and into shorts and t-shirts. Now we barely had to trim the sails and the boat was steady, sailing just off the wind in the direction of the Philippines.

This was a different world to anything I had experienced before. Surrounded by nothing but the ocean below and sky above, our whole environment and everything that mattered shrank down to the fifty feet onboard the boat. There really was nothing else to think or worry about. There were no distractions, no phones or TV, nothing to separate us from the wilderness of the ocean. I found myself more in tune with the wind and the weather, constantly scanning the horizon, looking out at the conditions ahead. Now, I began to notice everything in a slightly different way. I could feel the rhythm of the boat, I could sense if the wind slightly shifted, the waves changed or the clouds began to move differently.

At night, when I was at the helm, tethered to the cockpit, we could only see the inside of the boat and the sea was a dark mystery. *Purple X* was now our sanctuary, keeping us steady, keeping us safe. And everything on board, from the fresh water to the food, kept us alive. Without her we were nothing, we were lost. She cradled us, took care of us, and we looked after her, too. During the day I walked round the deck, inspecting the sails, keeping the galley clean and clear of obstructions, making the beds and generally ensuring everything was working as it should be. At that moment I experienced a feeling akin to love for our boat. I wanted to reach out, pat her on the side and say: 'Well done old girl.'

Hmmm… maybe we can do this. Maybe Raymond is right and we really can sail round the world.

2

WATCHING AIRPLANES

August 1977 – Lymm, Cheshire

Where are they going?
I squinted upwards as the tiny plane traced a white line across the pale sky. Our home in Cheshire lay under the edge of the flight path of Manchester Airport. As siblings, me, my twin Andrew and our younger sister Elizabeth took turns to mow our lawn so I was out here, pushing our heavy petrol mower up and down the large garden. I'd learned how to use the machine from a young age, filling up the tank, taking care not to spill any petrol from the jerry can, then pulling the starter cord hard enough to bring the engine chugging to life. We had moved to the property in Lymm, when I was seven years old. It could have been a beautiful garden but, like with our house, there just wasn't enough time or money to tend to it properly. Everything was overgrown and the weeds were out of control. My efforts to keep the lawn tidy was as much attention as our garden received, until I was older and could wield a garden fork and spade to dig the beds. My dad was too busy at work, my sister Elizabeth had her own chores and brother Andrew was usually out, roaming over the countryside with friends, up to his waist in lakes, grabbing tadpoles and frogs and hunting for rabbits.

I watched the plane heading off into the distance, leaving its track plumes disintegrating in the sky, forging a path towards some unknown destination. Leaving our shores, leaving this country behind.

I want to be on that plane. I want to be somewhere else, somewhere new, somewhere far away ... There's got to be more to life than living here like this.

But it was so high up, so far and out of reach, I could never imagine myself on that tiny plane. Our lives here were very much earth-bound, very much rooted to this little corner of England. Since our mother had left a year earlier, we had nothing but debts to our name. And a trip abroad seemed, well, impossible.

I must admit, it was a relief when our mother finally left. For years, she was unhappy and she didn't do anything to hide it. One night when I was eight years old, me and my siblings were woken by the sound of raised voices. We padded down the stairs of our old house in our night clothes and pushed open the living room door to see Mum screaming at Dad, and his face pouring with blood. On the floor beside him was a glass paperweight, one of those fashionable *objets d'art* my mother had insisted on buying for our mantelpiece. Dad was holding up a small coffee table as a shield. We knew in an instant what had happened; she had thrown it at his head, splitting his eye open. The bright red liquid now streaked the side of his face, onto his neck and collar.

'Please, Annette,' Dad begged my mother. 'Please just calm down. Please...'

We stood there, paralysed with fear. It was all so shocking. Dad spun around and saw the three of us standing outside the living room door.

'It's okay, it's okay, kids,' he tried to reassure us. 'Don't worry. Just go back upstairs. Go back to bed now.' Then he shut the door.

For a moment, none of us knew what to do. The whole scene

was horrifying – Dad with the blood on his face, his desperate pleas to my mother, begging her to calm down, her face contorted in anger. I felt tears sting my eyes. Elizabeth wept silently beside me, Andrew was too numb to speak. *What can we do? What can we do?* I knew something terrible was happening behind that door but I had no idea what we could do to stop it. We weren't allowed to use the phone and if we were, who would we call? What would we say? I felt lost and out of my depth. So we did as we were told. We ran back up the stairs and hid under our duvets. I shared a room with my five-year-old sister Elizabeth and we whispered to each other in the darkness: 'What do you think is happening?' 'Is Dad okay?' 'What's going on?'

It was my twin brother Andrew I felt most sorry for that night, he was in a room on his own.

It's hard to admit, but I never really liked my mum. Before moving to Cheshire we had lived in Wigan until Andrew and I were four. My earliest memory was of locking my mum out of the house. I'm not sure if I did it with any malicious intent, I really can't remember. But I do recall toddling towards the big, heavy back door after my mother had gone to the garden to hang some washing out, pushing the door closed and moving the iron bolt across. I couldn't have been more than four years old at the time. We moved to Stockton Heath on the outskirts of Warrington when Elizabeth was born in November 1966, to a large semi-detached, six bedroom Victorian house with an attic and a cellar. In Wigan we had lived in a modest, semi-detached house left to my dad by his father. It was a mortgage-free existence but Mum didn't like the idea of living in a house she hadn't chosen so she was soon on the hunt for a new place to live. Not long after our move to Stockton Heath, Mum got itchy feet again and started house hunting in the pretty village of Lymm in affluent Cheshire. There, our parents took on a four-bedroom detached house with a huge garden that overlooked fields both front and back.

My father worked as a warehouse manager for the wine and spirits trade in Liverpool while my mother worked full time as a personal assistant on the outskirts of Manchester. But she often had fallings out with colleagues so she bounced from one job to another. She was a vivacious woman, very lively and intelligent and good company in the right circumstances. Though at home, and to those who knew her well, she seemed in a state of permanent dissatisfaction. Certainly, her needs always came first. As a young child, I was plagued with frequent ear infections and perforated eardrums which left me partially deaf for several months at a time. This often caused me to speak loudly, which gave my classmates the impression I was rather bossy. One afternoon, as I lay on the sofa in our living room, sobbing from the pain, my mother eyed me crossly from her armchair facing the TV.

'Can't you just shut up?' she snapped. 'I'm trying to watch here. It's so annoying.'

'But it hurts. It hurts, Mummy,' I wept.

'Well, what do you want me to do about it?' she sighed. 'I've taken you to the doctor. You've got some antibiotics. What more can I do?'

Some sympathy or kindness would have been nice, but it appeared that this was too much to ask. There were many such instances when our needs as children were dismissed and diminished as no more than inconveniences to my mother. And then there were the other times, the moments of cruelty, that cut to the core.

When I was six years old, my sister and I were playing in the garden on the seesaw, bouncing up and down, when we heard the familiar tinkling music of the ice cream van coming down the road. We both jumped up as one, eager to get to the van before it

THE WATER RABBIT

moved off to another street and I asked Mum for change for an ice cream each. I was going to be very grown up and buy the ice creams on my own. She wasn't happy to do it – she rarely was – but I begged and eventually she relented, counting out the coins carefully into my palm. I put the money in the big pocket at the front of my sundress my Grandma had made for me and turned to my sister: 'Come on, Elizabeth, I'm going to buy the ice creams!'

We ran to the end of the garden, out the back gate, up the hill and towards a queue of kids outside the ice cream van. Patiently, we waited our turn and when we came to the front of the queue, I could barely reach over the counter.

'Two ice cream cornets, please,' I said loudly. The ice cream man made two and I put the coppers on the counter. He counted them out and frowned: 'Well, you don't have enough money.'

'I do have enough money,' I replied, adamant. 'My mum gave me the right money.'

'No, you only have enough money for one.' So he only gave me one.

There must be a mistake. What do I do? Since we only had one ice cream I didn't know if it belonged to me or Elizabeth. And as I had no more money I thought it best to take the ice cream back to Mum and ask her.

'Come on,' I said to Elizabeth. 'Let's go home.'

Now, as we ran back home the ice cream started to melt and dribble down my hand. I licked it off my knuckles, still clutching the cone as evidence of our predicament. At home Mum looked at us confused: 'Where's the other ice cream?'

'The thing is…' I started. 'There wasn't enough money. We only got this one. Something went wrong so what should we do with this?' And I held out the ice cream.

'Well, I'll tell you what we should do with this, you *selfish child*, only buying *one* ice cream!' She then plucked the cone out of my hand, pushed the ice cream into my face and rubbed it all over my face, hard. Then she threw it on the floor. I was too shocked to move but I felt myself crumbling inside. Elizabeth who was only about three, giggled a little, obviously thinking it was some silly game mum was playing with me.

My dad, Bob, was absolutely besotted with my mother and gave in to her every whim and demand. Anything to keep the peace. But it seemed nothing was ever enough for her and she tired of things very quickly. One minute she'd be bubbling over with ideas and excitement, the next she was fed up and walking away. When we first moved to our house in Lymm, my mother had grand ideas of how to improve the place, striding from room to room, sketching out the changes with her hands: 'We'll knock this through and make the lounge bigger. I want a new bathroom and the kitchen needs sorting. I don't like the walled courtyard round the patio, so that can all be knocked down. I want a porch on the front of the house. We'll take the banister off the stairs and open it up, the hall is too dark. The whole place needs fully redecorating....'

But once the builders moved in and started work on the renovations she got fed up, complaining frequently and loudly about the mess and disruption.

One day I was in the living room when I overheard a conversation with my Grandma, her mother.

'I can't take all this chaos anymore,' said Mum irritably. 'I've booked to go on holiday to the Amalfi Coast in Italy. Bob and I need to get away from all this building work.'

'What about the children?' asked Grandma

'No, they're not coming.'

'Who's going to look after them then?'

'You can,' my mother said curtly, 'You can move in and look

after them.'

'Well, I've got my house in Warrington and your Dad to look after,' Grandma replied, frowning. 'He goes to work every day.'

'Well, he can go to work from here,' Mum tutted. 'It's fine.'

It was a very odd conversation. Grandma didn't seem surprised by the unreasonable demand, but nonetheless still disappointed. My mother seemed to have no thought of how her actions might impact those around her – like my Grandma and Grandad not to mention me and my siblings — she simply didn't have a care of anybody else's needs. She did what she wanted and everybody had to like it or lump it.

Inevitably, perhaps, the marriage began to break down. It seemed no matter what my father did it was never enough and the fighting got worse and worse. At first we had no way of knowing this was abnormal. As a child you have no yardstick, no points of comparison, but I always felt very sorry for my father. He was an only child and an orphan, and there didn't seem to be anyone he could turn to for help or advice. He seemed out of his depth with my mother and though she meant the world to him, I don't think he had any idea of how to handle her frequent mood swings and impossible demands. Mum threatened suicide, she even took overdoses on a couple of occasions. I'm not sure she ever really meant to kill herself — she was always in hospital in time to have her stomach pumped – but there was no doubt she was unhappy in the marriage and suffering from undiagnosed mental illness.

In my first year of grammar school Mum was admitted to Winwick, the local psychiatric hospital. By then, I knew things weren't normal in our family. I'd visited a few friends' homes and noted their tidy houses and tidy lives. Our house seemed to be in a permanent state of disrepair and chaos. I tried my best to help. I was always picking things up, cleaning, hoovering, doing my best to make our house more comfortable but the building work stopped before it was completed and we lived amongst peeling wallpaper, unfinished and chipped walls. I have to admit, the rooms that were finished – like the living and dining rooms – were done well. Mum had a good eye for detail and added thoughtful touches which looked classy, like the plates hung in a slanting row up the staircase wall. I loved those. But she had lost interest in day-to-day housekeeping and Dad just didn't have the time, so our house was messy and uncared for. We children were also left to fend for ourselves. I made my own breakfast and walked to school each morning, popping by my friend's house to pick her up on the way. There, I noticed her mum was at home making breakfast, everything always appeared to be in good order, and there was an easiness between the family members. Nobody here seemed brittle, ready to fracture at any moment.

One morning, when I stopped to pick up my friend, her mother asked how my mum was, as people do in normal conversation. Unthinkingly, I replied 'My mum's in hospital.'

The mother and father glanced at one another, concerned.

'Oh dear. I'm so sorry to hear that, Carolyn,' said the mother. 'Which hospital is she in?'

I started to panic. I didn't want to say Winwick – everyone knew it was the psychiatric hospital and I didn't want them to think my mother was a lunatic. I felt myself flush with shame.

'Erm… she's in this hospital just off the M62…' I muttered, looking down at the floor. 'But, well, I've forgotten the name of it.' I felt so self-conscious at that moment, about my mother, my situation, my reality, about the life we lived. It seemed so different from the lives of everyone else I knew.

Elizabeth, Andrew and I weren't told much about what went on in that hospital. They didn't in those days – adults talked in hushed tones behind closed doors, while children were ushered away, shielded from the truth. I'm not sure it really helped. Kids know when something is wrong and perhaps it's better to be open, to prevent the imagination filling in the gaps. Years later, I learned she had undergone electric shock treatment at Winwick, but at the time we weren't even allowed to visit her there.

'Your mum isn't well,' my Grandma would tell me. 'But don't worry. She'll be home soon and everything will be fine.'

When she did eventually come home, nothing seemed any better. She was still unhappy, she ran up a lot of debts and argued frequently with my dad about money. She had £80 a month housekeeping allowance for food and bills – the equivalent to around £400 a week in today's money, but always complained it wasn't enough. My Grandma was horrified by my mother's extravagance. She had lived through the war and never wasted a penny. Her comments about profligacy were interpreted as an attack on my mother's personality and she in turn accused my Grandma of living in the past.

'Life is there to be enjoyed!' my mum declared. 'Bob is earning good money. Why shouldn't we spend it?'

My father had been promoted to management level after much encouragement from my mum. Believing this a personal victory, Mum thought she deserved to enjoy the fruits of her persuasion, but whatever he gave her, it was never enough. Looking back on the money she spent and the things she bought, it was clear she was trying to buy happiness.

Gradually, she started living a separate life, going out to nightclubs late at night, meeting other men. Though we were still under the same roof, she no longer shared a bed with Dad. In fact, they didn't share anything anymore. We were like living like lodgers in a hostel. Previously, we'd had a living room and a dining room downstairs but my mother turned the dining room into her own living room and that was where she sat at night.

She also kept a separate shelf in the fridge for her own food and was rarely in the same room as my father. My dad now looked after the three of us — shopping, cooking and washing – while also holding down a full time job, while Mum did her own thing. I don't recall her spending time with us, taking us out, putting us to bed or even making us tea. She would only do what suited her and we didn't suit her. Whilst Dad at work, we were on our own, especially during school holidays, from the time Andrew and I were 10 and Elizabeth was seven.

We tried our best to muddle through in this strange new situation but it was a strain on all of us, particularly my father. Andrew stayed away as much as possible, out roaming the countryside all hours of the day and night, while Elizabeth and I tried to help with the housework. We talked late into the night in our shared bedroom about how odd and unsettling it all was. I knew they weren't happy and I longed to say something but could never find the right words. I had so many questions, but what to ask? Did my dad even have any answers?

When I was twelve, I remember one night my mother had a couple of girlfriends over and they were in bright spirits, putting on their makeup in the living room before going out to a nightclub. They were gossiping and laughing, taking it in turns to stand in front of the mirror to apply their make-up and I joined in the fun, trying on lipstick as I half-listened to their excitable chatter. Then, after they departed in a clattering of heels and clouds of perfume, I went to the other living room to sit with my dad. The room was pitch black and my father sat staring morosely at the television. I couldn't be certain because I couldn't see his face clearly, but I felt pretty sure he'd been crying.

'Oh, you've not got any lights on, Dad,' I spoke into the darkness. 'Shall I put them on?'

'No, it's okay,' he replied sadly. 'Just leave them.'

THE WATER RABBIT

The difference couldn't have been starker. My mother had moved on, she was already living another life. My father was alone and devastated, a broken man. They were sharing a house, but no longer sharing a life. Just coexisting. This was devastating to watch.

This went on for several months, until one morning when my dad came to our room to wake us up for school. It was unusual to see him at this time because he usually left the house early to travel to Liverpool.

'You need to get up,' he said gently.

'Yeah, okay…' I replied, stretching my arms over my head.

He lingered a little in the doorway.

'And, erm, by the way, your mum's left,' he added.

Thank God! I thought, letting out a huge sigh. I didn't know where she had gone and at this point, things were so bad, it came as a relief. It was as if I'd been holding my breath for months now and I could finally exhale. Now at least we could get our house back to the way it was before. We could use all the shelves in the fridge. We could turn her living room back into a dining room again. There would be no more separation! Over time, Andrew retreated more into himself and stayed out longer with his mates. Elizabeth and I took up the household chores and made the house as homey as possible,.

Still, it was a bleak time. Mum left us during the Winter of Discontent in 1978/79 when the miners strikes were going on. There were power cuts across the country and we were on a three-day week to preserve coal supplies. My sister, who was still at primary school, would come home from school as it was getting dark and let herself into the house but she wasn't allowed to turn anything on until me or my brother got home. She wasn't even tall enough to reach the keyhole on the front door so dad had modified the key by putting a length of metal rod through the hole of the Yale key at the top. This way she could use it as a lever to turn the key and the door would open. She'd sit there in the gloom until I came back and turned the gas fire on. Then we'd all huddle round it, trying to keep warm. It was the only light and the only source of heat in the house. There was no electricity, no television, all the power was off to conserve energy.

The power was only on for two hours each night, just enough time for Dad to cook us dinner on the electric cooker after he got home from work. Then, when the power went off again, we had a small camping light to read by. Ours wasn't a very welcoming home so I didn't invite anyone back. Besides, I didn't have many friends. I was timid, skinny and self-conscious, aware that our straightened circumstances were at odds with the affluent households in our area.

Mum had run up huge debts before she left. The bill from the milkman alone was £200, an enormous sum back in the seventies, equivalent to around £1,000 today. My father had no idea that she had stopped paying the bills some months before and for a while, it seemed a new bill arrived daily: from the butchers, the greengrocers, clothes catalogues, furniture stores. It was a mountain of debt and it all fell to my father. We three children continued to live in the house with him after my mum left – there was never a question of living with her – but during the divorce, my mum was awarded half the value of the house. Given the option of either taking it straight away or waiting till my younger sister Elizabeth was 18 and ready to leave home, she chose to take the money. So now Dad had to remortgage the house to pay her off, leaving him with even more debt, while he also bore the costs of our care. My mother, meanwhile, started her life afresh with a new man.

We were broke and for several years after she left, our summer holidays were taken in a tent in a farmer's field in North

THE WATER RABBIT

Wales. Dad couldn't even afford the tent, it was Grandma who paid for it, knowing we would have no holiday otherwise. Each summer, whatever the weather, we trooped up to Aberdaron in North Wales to set up camp in a farmer's field that was rutted with furrows from tractors tyres. We tried to make the best of it, sleeping under canvas and on bumpy ground at night, playing badminton on sunnier days, but our ankles kept disappearing into the deep, ploughed furrows. None of us complained, of course, we all knew our father was doing his best as a single parent. But the idea of getting on a plane or going abroad was just beyond anything I could imagine. Still, I liked to look up sometimes when I was mowing the lawn and imagine myself somewhere else. Somewhere far away from Lymm.

3

CHRISTMAS IN THE PHILIPPINES

24 December, 2007

DAY FIVE ONBOARD, we pulled together as a team. It was slightly surprising to me – especially since I'd had so many anxieties over our trip – but as a crew we were in tune with one another, everything ran like clockwork and everyone knew what they were meant to be doing. There were no arguments about who was meant to be on watch, we all just stuck to the rota and did our bit. It helped that out at sea, there were no distractions – no TV or phones – instead we talked, shared stories, joked and passed the time as we might have done in the days before non-stop entertainment took over our lives. And before Raymond's Blackberry took over his. There was something relaxing too about having all the children onboard. For the first time in years, they weren't scattered in various parts of the world, and knowing where they were at all times gave me a lot of comfort.

Guided by the elements, we were also in tune with our physical environment, enjoying each sunrise and sunset, at one with nature, respectful of it. Being on watch as dawn was breaking was wonderful; steering the yacht into another day, noticing the sky and seeing what clues the clouds or the shades of pink or gold may offer as to how the weather would be. The nearer we got to the Philippines, the more we knew we were in for sunny days and blue skies. Twilight too had a different feel. As the sun went down and the temperature dipped, it was like entering a new world. I loved the deeper shade of rich indigo as twilight faded and we were on the cusp of the pure black of night. We saw occasional phosphorescence along the side of the boat and in her trail, the sparkling glow of turquoise caused by the yacht moving through the water.

At night, we enjoyed both cloudy and clear skies and noted the stark difference between the two. With cloud cover there was total blackness. On a clear night, the glow of the moon was a strong beacon when we were surrounded by darkness. As the stars appeared and shifted across the sky, I felt the excitement of seeing this in a new way, far away from land. The stars gave me a glimpse of our place in the universe, if only for a few short hours. The steady presence of billions of years of lights, floating down, ageless, timeless, existing well beyond our lives, limits and imagination. Here there was no light pollution, no steady ground underfoot. I felt the gentle rise and fall as *Purple X* ploughed through the sea. This connection to nature and distance from human activity was a revelation that I could not have imagined had I not experienced it for myself

We had taken some great holidays and seen fantastic natural sights, glaciers and geysers in New Zealand, the Great Barrier Reef, The Alps and the constellations in the southern hemisphere. Yet from our yacht, the vastness of sea and sky gave a different perspective. *We really are very small creatures*, I marvelled, appreciating just how far we had ventured beyond the footprint of human activity. One night the moon came out and we were blanketed by a vast, star-filled skyscape above us. It was utterly magical being out on the boat on a moon-lit sea, black waves illuminated by the silver speckled sky. The trip was better than I had envisaged! The boat was steady and I felt we were a capable and accomplished team.

By now meals became the focus of our day and I made sure we all came together to enjoy hearty food full of sustenance to keep our energy levels up. Then, we would briefly turn on the autopilot, setting the navigation and the sails to manage themselves, so we could let go the wheel, sit down and eat in the cockpit together. That was the sense we had at all times – we were together, unified, a team. Nobody was unfairly burdened or left to manage one job. For our whole time at sea, the shifts changed, ensuring we all took it in turns to clear up, wash up and go on watch. Everybody just helped, taking it in turns to do what was needed.

As the weather improved and we spent more time on deck, I found myself slipping into a different state of being. I'd never undertaken a journey where so much of our trip was in our own hands. We had gone on long car trips before but there was always a road, a way ahead laid out in front of us. At sea it was just us and the boat. We had to go with the wind, adjusting our course and sails to the vagaries of the weather. We had to take note of how the elements were guiding us and make our plans accordingly. It felt like we were operating on a different plane, in harmony with our surroundings, surrendering to forces greater than ourselves. I could see, for the first time in years, how tiny we were in relation to the vastness of the ocean. Out at sea, petty worries seemed to fall away and the things I fretted about at home now seemed small and irrelevant. Nothing in the world mattered beyond our boat and staying on course. My whole focus narrowed down to the time and space we now occupied.

The days passed quickly because we were always busy: busy thinking about the next meal, busy preparing it, eating it, clearing it, resting, making the beds, going out on watch, cleaning the bathrooms, or writing in the log. Keeping the log was good protocol so whoever was on watch would make a note of what the weather was doing, the distance we'd covered, our progress and anything we saw or passed at sea. Occasionally we caught sight of the odd ship on the horizon, and as we neared the Philippines we saw a few fishing boats, but nothing terribly exciting. Nevertheless, we kept our eyes on the ocean, noting down everything we saw in the log. The four-hour watch system disrupted our sleep patterns so in the afternoons we often snoozed or read. Hannah took long, languid catnaps on deck while topping up her tan, the boys tried fishing, though they didn't catch anything as the water was too deep, Paul was an avid reader and spent his downtime catching up on historical seafaring novels, while Lars – who worked in banking, like Raymond – caught up on lost sleep. Raymond's job was taking a large toll on him and as a result, our relationship was suffering for it In the evenings we swapped sailing stories and Martin held the kids enraptured, describing his tours of duty in Iraq and Beirut.

I have to say that onboard Raymond was easier to be around. Away from the stresses of his work he relaxed more and shouted less. I sensed, too, that he appreciated all my efforts to ensure that our trip was a success: preparing the yacht, the paperwork and all the provisions. Together, on the boat, Raymond and I were calm, accomplished and focused and for the first time in a long while I felt we worked effectively as a team. So on Christmas Eve, when we pulled into Subic Bay, Philippines the whole crew stood a little taller, a little prouder than before, enjoying a real sense of achievement in taking ourselves from one country to another on our own skills. During five days at sea, we had navigated our way across hundreds of miles of ocean and that was no small thing. Now we had finally reached our destination.

As we motored past a couple of naval ships, we were reminded to steer well clear by the flashing buoys and the warning signs telling us to keep a distance. Subic Bay, had been an American naval base until 1991 and though there were now many pleasure boats moored up, there were also military vessels, allowed to berth for limited periods of time. We found a visitors berth and moored *Purple X*, pleased to be on a pontoon as it would make for easy access on and off the boat.

That night we decorated the boat ahead of Christmas Day, stringing up purple fairy lights around the yacht and hanging red and white candy canes from the boom. Finally, it was time to open the champagne.

'To the crew of *Purple X*!' I held my champagne flute in the air and we all clinked glasses.

What an achievement! After five days at sea and without a drink, the cold bubbles had their desired effect and a warm, satisfied feeling spread upwards to my glowing, sunburnt cheeks. It wasn't long before we were all feeling very merry – and incredibly tired! Now, instead of going to sleep in their cabins, Martin and Hannah chose to take advantage of the warm weather and sleep on deck in the open cockpit, using the made-to-measure cushions as makeshift mattresses. Raymond and I slept in the master cabin as usual, while Paul, Lars and our sons, Aaron and Joe, spread themselves around the saloon and two other cabins. For the first time in five days we all looked forward to a peaceful and lengthy sleep, no weather to worry about, no watch system. Safe in harbour and peaceful. Of course, there was a bit of tidying to do after five days at sea but that could all wait until we had caught up on our sleep.

'Mmmmm, something smells good,' I said appreciatively as I sniffed the sizzling bacon in the air. On Christmas morning the kids treated us to a full English breakfast – eggs, bacon, black pudding, the lot. It was a magnificent start to the day and afterwards I gave out small gifts – a book each for Martin, Lars, Paul and the children. Raymond and I didn't often give each other gifts these days. We would just buy what we wanted as and when needed. Then we waited for immigration officials to arrive and check us into the country. The previous evening we'd called the yacht club to let them know we had made it safely into berth and they contacted immigration on our behalf. I have to admit, I found it a little odd when the two officials climbed aboard the boat in the late morning and immediately requested a beer each. Raymond and I looked at each other and shrugged — *well, it IS Christmas!* – so I retrieved the beers and handed over our passports at the same time. The officials pulled open their cans and took long swigs, barely glancing at the passports. They seemed to be waiting for something.

'Erm, is there anything else we need to do?' I asked.

'That'll be 200 dollars, US,' said one official. I raised a quizzical eyebrow at Raymond. As far as I was aware there was no fee for immigration, and the sum requested didn't really match anything with regards a tariff chart. He appeared to have plucked a random number from thin air. But Raymond nodded – what else could we do? – and I went to our locker to get the money. Fortunately, Paul, who had sailed into the Philippines many times before and knew the drill, had prepared us for this possibility and we had plenty of cash onboard.

'Do I get a receipt for that?' I asked, as the official counted out the notes.

'No, that's just what you pay,' he said gruffly.

Of course, I thought. *They wouldn't want any record of this exchange.*

After they left, we all disembarked to the yacht club, where we used the Wi-Fi to check messages from friends and family. Then we ventured out into town to find a restaurant and later,

Hannah, myself and Martin took advantage of the club facilities to enjoy a massage each. That afternoon we also paid a visit to a go-kart track and raced each other round and round. I came last, of course! I didn't mind – I was a cautious driver and not interested in vying for top position. That night we rigged up the DVD player on the yacht and watched the James Bond movie *Casino Royale*. I have to say that it felt like a very special Christmas. There was nothing traditional about it whatsoever but we were on holiday in the Philippines, I had all my family with me and the whole day was utterly unique. Everyone was enjoying themselves. Paul teased Raymond and remarked that he had stopped shouting as previously had been the case on other trips to Macau. Raymond had a habit of yelling things such as *'Fuck sake pull the main sheet in.'* I pointed out that instruction was rather vague, as who was *'Fucksake'*? Joe with his dry sense of humour, says it's not a problem for me, I'm known as *'Jesus Christ'*. We all laughed, but it was a reminder of how stressful things could get when instructions were given.

On Boxing Day we decided to slip the lines and sail round to a neighbouring beach where we anchored up and Hannah and I attempted to make French fries, shallow frying cut potatoes in cooking oil. After lunch we dived off the boat and swam to the beach. There was no one around on the empty, white sandy beach, surrounded by overgrown vegetation and it felt for all the world as if we had discovered a secret hidden gem. We all pottered about and in the Robinson Crusoe spirit. The kids asked Martin to show them how to light a fire by rubbing sticks together, though not too successfully as there was no dry driftwood lying about. Back on board, Joe climbed the mast and took a bird's eye photo of us swimming around the yacht. Another a great day out and we'd not even left the comfort of our mobile home!

The following day Martin complained of an ear problem

so we all trekked to town in search of a doctor. The place was festooned with Christmas decorations and I noticed everyone we met appeared very happy. This wasn't a rich or glamorous place like Hong Kong. In fact, like much of South East Asia, the Philippines is a country of struggles, suffering frequent natural disasters of earthquakes, typhoons, floods and volcanoes. Their largest export is human labour. There are large numbers of domestic helpers, mainly women, who live and work in Hong Kong. The money they could earn in one year there was a fortune compared to what they could earn during the same time in the Philippines. But it was a hard life. The women, often mothers, were separated from their families to work overseas for years at a time and they were often exploited. Certain rights were now legally enshrined in Hong Kong law and these hard-working, economic exiles were entitled to a trip home every two years at the end of each contract so they could be reunited with their loved ones, if only for a few weeks.

However, back home in the Philippines, corruption was a means of survival for many living hand-to-mouth, both at the official level and within smaller, domestic settings. We had had our own small taste of this on arrival in the country. Our own wonderful helper Melinda was Filipino and she said it was impossible to ship anything home unless she herself was there to receive it. All personal items were rifled through first by custom officials, and then by her extended family. So by the time she got home, there would be nothing left of the original package.

But this wasn't an issue to mar our trip to the Philippines, where the unspoilt beaches and friendly locals made it a very welcoming place to visit. Plus, we had arrived at the best time of year! Christmas was a very big deal here and now we could feel joy and happiness everywhere. Jolly carols blared out from radios in many of the shops and colourful decorations hung from every available space.

'We start putting up our decorations up on July 1,' joked one shop owner when we noted the abundance of festive décor.

Raymond and I found a doctor who confirmed that Martin had an ear infection and prescribed antibiotics, then we spent the rest of the afternoon wandering around the shops, buying provisions for the journey back, and enjoying the atmosphere and sights of the town. Back on the boat I got all the bedding and clothes laundered and, after dinner, the whole crew headed to a small nightclub where we knocked back cocktails and took it in turns to strut our stuff on the dance floor.

On 28 December, four days after our arrival, Hannah and Lars flew back to Hong Kong. Lars had promised his girlfriend he would be back in time to celebrate New Year's Eve together, while Hannah would be going to a New Year's Eve party and then on to France for a skiing trip with her university friends. I was pleased they were returning together since I knew it could be dangerous for a young girl to travel round the Philippines on her own. Accompanied by Lars, however, Hannah would be safe. The pair boarded a small plane from Subic Bay to Manila and we waved them off as they flew over the harbour. From there they would pick up a flight into Hong Kong. We were due to leave ourselves the following day to get back in Hong Kong just after the New Year.

That afternoon Raymond and I got chatting to Victor in the Marina, and discovered he was a 'boat boy', working on another yacht. (The term *boat boy* here is a slightly misleading one. Victor was in his thirties and certainly no 'boy' but this was the commonly used phrase among the sailing community.) The owner of Victor's boat was away for Christmas, leaving him nothing to do. Although I knew we could probably manage fine with just six of us aboard, I recalled our discussions with Oyster about taking on a professional crew for our proposed trip around the world. This could be a good opportunity to work with a professional crewman, so Raymond made Victor a proposition, offering to pay him to sail with us and then fly him back to the Philippines after we docked. Victor agreed to the deal and came onboard the next morning with just a small rucksack, the sum total of all his worldly goods.

The night of the 28th, before we were due to leave, we befriended the skipper of a large boat run by the Hong Kong chapter of the global adventure sports group, Outward Bound. They had pulled into Subic Bay a couple of days earlier with eleven people on board, four professional crew and seven novices who had sailed over with them but were now disembarking in Subic Bay. Discussing our plans to return to Hong Kong, we all got to talking about the weather. That was normal for anyone who sailed – the weather was a constant preoccupation – but it was even more critical than usual because, around Hong Kong at this time of year, there was a monsoon that cycled every five days, and we were about to head into the open ocean. If we sailed during the five-day gap of this monsoon, conditions were stable, but if we caught the edge of it, the going could get a little rough. The Outward Bound skipper said he wasn't yet ready to leave. They had hit a random wave on the way over, causing the locker lid inside the cockpit to fly off, smacking one of their professional crewmen on the head. Now he was in hospital in town.

'We're a crew member down,' the skipper said. 'And I'm not going back short-handed.'

'That's understandable,' I said. They were on a 67-foot yacht, and a boat that size would ideally need all four professional crew on board. I thought now of the 62-foot yacht we had on order; that was a lot of boat and a lot of responsibility.

'We're planning on leaving tomorrow,' I said. 'Seven of us,

and six of us can sail.'

The skipper thought for a moment, then said: 'Well, with a yacht like yours and the number of people you have, it won't be a problem.'

That was reassuring to hear, especially from an experienced sailor.

The next morning we were all up early to read the weather reports and have one last discussion about our planned departure. Though we could see there might be some choppiness ahead, we weren't expecting hurricane force winds. This time we would be beating into the wind, that is, sailing with the wind in front of us instead of sailing with the wind at our back, as we did on the way over. Most people preferred sailing downwind since it was usually very calm and as long as the wind remained behind you, you were stable. But beating into the wind meant chopping into it, giving a bumpier ride. Actually, I quite liked sailing upwind. I found it easier to trim the sails and manoeuvre the boat. I felt we had more control. At times with the wind behind you, a sudden wind shift could cause you to gybe, or 'change course', sending the massive boom swinging in an uncontrolled arc across the cockpit. That was dangerous, bad for the rigging and something to be avoided. However, during this crossing we would have the wind in front of us and so it was decided, we would leave as planned.

As we powered up the engine to leave Subic Bay, I knew we were more than equipped to deal with any bumpiness ahead. The bad weather further out to sea was a Force 6 on the Beaufort scale, giving a wind speed of between 22 to 27 knots, a steady breeze for a boat of our size. We knew what serious wind was like as we had sailed in a Force 8 – 42 knots – so this would be fairly manageable in comparison. I had my concerns, of course. There was always a certain measure of apprehension when sailing into the weather instead of away from it. But the voyage on the way over had given me confidence and I knew we were a strong, capable team. Yes, it might get a little bumpy out there but nothing we couldn't handle. Nothing we hadn't seen before.

4

RAYMOND

January 1985, The Wirral

'IT'S RAYMOND...' Eamon said when he trotted back up the stairs of the townhouse. 'He wants to know if anybody wants to go to the pub.'

Oh, so this must be Raymond who takes Eamon and Karen to work every morning in his car.

At 21, I was working as a manager at M&S in Birkenhead and my friend and colleague Fiona shared a house with Eamon and Karen. We were often in and out of each other's houses and I was aware the pair worked with a bloke called Raymond at Royal Insurance because they talked a lot about him... A LOT! It was always *'Raymond this, Raymond that'* so naturally, I was curious to meet this Raymond fellow. When the doorbell rang in the early evening Eamon went down to answer and we all agreed a trip to the pub would be a great idea. So Raymond came upstairs into the living room.

'Hi, I'm Raymond,' he smiled warmly. *Raymond is Chinese!* I was a bit taken aback. *Why hadn't anyone thought to tell me he was Chinese?* Of course, it didn't really matter one way or another, but it took me by surprise at first and he looked particularly Chinese since he was wearing a quilted jacket with a Mandarin collar. It's not like we lived in a particularly ethnically diverse area, so Raymond stood out straight away. I introduced myself, then we all trooped off to the pub up the road. I didn't really talk much to Raymond that first night at the pub, but I was intrigued by this smartly dressed, well-spoken young man who appeared so different from everyone else I knew.

I had moved out of home a year after starting the M&S management training scheme, which I joined straight after my A Levels at school. Despite my worries, I had done pretty well in my exams and, in line with my grammar school's expectations, I had dutifully filled out the UCCA form to apply to study Biology at university. It was the usual and well-trodden path of high-achieving students and my father, too, was keen for me to fulfil my 'academic potential'. But as I stared at the form, carefully written in black pen as directed, a thought popped into my head: 'I'm not going to go.' It suddenly struck me that I wasn't interested in going to university. At that moment all I wanted was to take control of my life. *I'm sick of living without money and trying to please everybody. Do I really want to spend another three years of my life getting into debt?* I ripped up the UCCA form then and there and decided instead to apply to the M&S management training scheme which I'd heard about through my friend. I was concerned about Dad's reaction at first. But his disappointment was quickly allayed when I landed a place on the prestigious, well-paid scheme. He was reassured then that I wasn't throwing my life away.

As for my mother, she didn't care one way or another. After she left home she went to live with her new partner, who she later married in a large house on the outskirts of Manchester. We three kids were made to spend one weekend a month with her there. Sadly, this was never a particularly enjoyable experience, especially later on as he became an alcoholic. My mother talked endlessly about herself, her plans to redecorate and her holidays to Europe. She never asked about us or seemed interested in our lives, let alone invited us along on her holidays abroad. When I told her I was worried about taking my O-Levels she batted away my concerns with: 'Oh well, it's just a few exams, isn't it?'

My brother didn't see the point of the visits and stopped going to see her, but Elizabeth and I hung in, if truth be told, for our own material interest. If we didn't have the money for a new dress, Mum would sometimes buy one for us. Or she might take us to the cinema, a luxury we could never afford ourselves. It sounds selfish now but in the end we only went there for what we could get out of her. Besides, I'd learned not to talk about the things that mattered to me. What was the point when she never expressed any interest? By the time I was making my own way in the world, she had already moved down south and I saw much less of her.

At eighteen, I was happy to be earning my own money, but expectations were high and in those days, senior management were not slow at pointing out mistakes or giving critical reviews. Nevertheless, I knew I'd made the right choice when all my mates came back from university at Christmas of that first year, complaining of how much debt they were in and how much they'd drunk at various parties. *Well, if that is what university is about I'm happy to give it a miss*, I thought to myself. I'd spent my whole life to that point in debt and I'd had enough of it.

During my first year of training at the store in Warrington, I commuted from home, but after transferring to Birkenhead I moved into a shared house on The Wirral. Now I had my own car, my own money and my own home, though I was still close to my dad and saw him frequently at the weekends. A month after meeting Raymond, Dad came for a visit and we were just sitting down to a cup of tea when the doorbell rang. I ran down the stairs to open the door and was surprised to see Raymond standing there, holding a beautiful arrangement of red roses in a vase with a card tucked inside.

'Oh, hello!' I exclaimed. It was only the second time I had ever set eyes on him.

'Hi Carolyn,' he said. 'I hope you don't mind, Fiona gave me your address. It's Valentine's Day so I just thought I'd like to give you these flowers.'

I thanked him, took the flowers, then went back upstairs to see my dad.

'Those are nice,' he noted.

'Hmm....' I replied, plucking the card out and opening the envelope. It was an invitation to dinner. *Well, why not?* I thought. *A girl's got to eat.*

A few weeks later Raymond took me to a nice restaurant in Liverpool and we talked for hours. I was fascinated to learn about his unusual background. Raymond was from a prominent Chinese family who had fled to Hong Kong when the communists took over in 1949. His grandfather had ten wives – which was commonplace back then – and Raymond's father was born to wife number ten. Over the years, the large family had splintered across the continents. Raymond's parents moved to the UK, sending him and his sister to private boarding schools here, and supporting themselves with a Chinese takeaway in Runcorn. Now Raymond was 28, seven years older than me, spoke with an impeccable British accent, held two degrees and appeared quite the most sophisticated and smartest person I'd ever met.

He casually dropped into conversation that he was going to Toronto for the weekend to visit a relative. *For the weekend!* I marvelled. *Who does that?* I was intrigued by this man... for a girl with so little experience beyond this small corner of England, he seemed remarkably exotic. And his family set-up was a world away from anything I had ever experienced. At the weekends, they all got together in their family home, where there were often lots of cousins staying, family members living over here, away from their parents, to access the British private school system. It was all a new and bizarre concept to me that I couldn't quite get my head around — this huge family helping each other out on so many different levels.

After that first date we started to see each other regularly. Raymond was so different from everyone else I knew; suave, self-assured, he was clearly a man going places. His first degree was in Architecture and his second was in Maths and Statistics. Now he worked as an actuary and I could tell that he was both fiercely intelligent and just as ambitious. Raymond represented something else that I found deeply attractive – the possibility of something more. All my life I'd yearned for a bigger life, something beyond my world. I had taken a couple of trips abroad when I was at school – one to Rome and another to Russia, when my dad could scrape the money together. He had wanted to show me something of the world outside Cheshire, to open my horizons and to give me the experiences he felt I missed out on because of our lack of funds. Seeing the way people lived in other countries had inflamed my desire to travel. And with Raymond, I was certain this would happen.

There was just one fly in the ointment – Raymond's mother. The moment she found out he was dating a non-Asian girl for a couple of months, she was incensed.

'If you see that girl again, you're dead to me!' she threatened him. I was shocked to be rejected because of my race in my own country; besides, we were only dating at this stage. Raymond refused to let his mother dictate his love life and I was touched by his loyalty, standing up for me against his family, even though we had only known each other a few months at that point. But when his mother found out we were still dating she burned every item of his in the family house, even his childhood photos. It was dramatic, to say the least.

'Asian families are a bit complicated,' Raymond's sister tried to explain one day. Justine was five years younger than Raymond and two years older than me. *Complicated?*! I thought. *You don't have to tell me about complicated families!* I'd been through plenty of dramas of my own. Still, I very much wanted to be part of Raymond's and hoped that his mother would relent.

'Do you think she'll come round?' I asked Justine.

'Yes, I'm sure she will. We have our own ways of doing things. It just takes time.'

In any case, Raymond was undeterred by his mother's objections. He seemed besotted with me and that was a wonderful feeling. By early summer we travelled to Asia, visiting Singapore, Kuala Lumpur and Hong Kong. It was my first time in Asia so it was a lot to take in all in one go. Singapore was hot and humid and though we toured the city and I tried all the different foods, I felt quite overwhelmed at times. Malaysia felt more relaxed as we met up with a lot of Raymond's old university friends who were very welcoming, but I couldn't help feeling a little inadequate since they were all older than me and had clearly led very privileged lives in large houses with lots of domestic help. They talked and joked a lot about the 'old days' when they were all studying together in London and were kind enough to take us out, visiting tourist sites and joining us for dinner. I was pleased that Raymond had such strong relationships with the people he'd shared a special time with at university. I wasn't enamoured with Hong Kong. Clearly, Raymond's family there had been given the heads-up by his mother and their reaction was far from welcoming. His university friends seemed nice enough, but I'd had starry visions of Hong Kong as 'the Pearl of the Orient' and it fell far short of my expectations. In fact, it seemed to me a brutal and materialistic place. All the conversation with his family or friends revolved around money and seemed to have an angle of making one feel less than successful, depending what car you were driving, how much you earned, who you worked for and what you did at work.

We returned to the UK at the end of the month and both returned to our jobs. In September, one day we took a trip to Southport beach after work. It was getting late, already twilight, and the tide was far out when we pulled up.

'Let's get out the car to have a little walk on the sand,' suggested Raymond.

'What do you want to do that for?' I wasn't too bothered about getting out of the car.

'Look, it's getting dark.'

'Come on...' he urged so, reluctantly, I obliged. We started walking along the sand when suddenly Raymond turned to me and got down on one knee. Out of nowhere it seemed he produced a bunch of pink roses. I was delighted but very surprised, after only six months of dating. How had he kept those secret?

'Carolyn, I love you so much...' He retrieved a little box from his coat pocket and opened it up. Inside shimmered a stunning, solitaire diamond ring. 'Will you marry me?'

I couldn't believe it. We had talked a little about being together during our trip abroad, sharing our hopes and dreams, but the proposal still came as a surprise.

'Yes!' I laughed. 'Yes, I will.'

I was thrilled. Raymond had done it all very traditionally, he had even rung my dad to ask his permission first and I was over the moon. Raymond offered me everything I wanted in life: stability and dependability combined with excitement and the opportunity for new experiences. Getting married felt like the right thing to do.

THE WATER RABBIT

We planned our wedding for Saturday 21 June 1986, the longest day of the year. I chose it especially because I wanted the day to last as long as possible. Neither of us was brought up in any particular religion but we decided to get married in the Baptist Chapel near where I had grown up as I had started attending the church during my sixth form years, joining a couple of religious friends there. Dad wasn't happy about it at the time. I think he would have preferred for me to go drinking at the local pub rather than spend my Sunday evenings at the Baptist church, but I found it interesting. I went to a few Bible study groups, met some genuinely lovely people and learned something about the more spiritual side of life.

In the run up to our wedding, we had regular meetings with our church leader, who counselled us in the different aspects of marriage. I felt it was important for us to lay the right foundations and during these pre-marriage counselling sessions we tackled big questions, like how we intended to raise our children, what would we do if we had to make big decisions and how we saw our lives as a married couple. These were really helpful to me; my parents' marriage, after all, was not one I wished to replicate. It was during one of these sessions that my mother came up in conversation. By this point, I was barely speaking to her and had no intention of inviting her to the wedding. She had moved down to Buckinghamshire and was on her own again after splitting from her second husband. We had never been close but when she found out I was getting married she called up in tears, distressed by my decision to leave her out of the wedding plans.

'Why are you doing this to me?' she wept. 'My own daughter! How cruel! Why can't I be there? I won't make any fuss, I promise. I just want to witness you in the church and then I'll slip away...'

We were already estranged from Raymond's mother and though I was worried about my own mother causing a scene,

I was aware that if she wasn't invited to our wedding, our relationship may never recover. Losing two mothers was a daunting prospect and our church leader suggested that an invitation could be a chance to reset our relationship, ensuring there were no bad feelings between us in the future. So, despite my misgivings, I relented and invited her to join us.

'Look, Mum, it's just the ceremony at 10.30 a.m. and then a trip on the coach to the lunch reception,' I explained. 'We're having a Chinese banquet in a Chester restaurant and that's it. It's not a whole evening thing, there's no disco, but if you want to come you can come for the day.'

A couple of weeks before the big day she rang in tears again.

'I'm sitting here crying because I haven't got any money,' she sobbed. 'I just want to look nice on your wedding day and I'm trying to cobble together something to make a hat but it's so hard...'

I sighed: 'Okay, how much money do you want?'

Sadly, and just as I had feared, it was just the start of my mother's dramas. The night before the wedding she turned up on my doorstep, demanding to see my dress. I sent her away, telling her she would see it at the church with everyone else. The next day she kicked off in the church when she was not asked to sign the register, and even made a scene when we had the photos taken. It was one thing after another. At the restaurant she got upset because she wasn't on our table and she even complained when I gave my bouquet to Raymond's sister instead of her. It was maddening. She'd begged to come to the wedding and promised not to make a scene but just as I had feared she piled one drama on top of another, miserable every step of the way that it wasn't as she wanted it to be. *This isn't your wedding*, I wanted to scream at her. *This is supposed to be my special day. For once in your life, can you stop thinking of yourself. You're doing nothing but causing trouble and angst.*

As for Raymond's family, his father and sister were there but his mother made a pointed visit to Hong Kong during our nuptials. And for as long as we were married, she never spoke to Raymond again. Still, somehow, we enjoyed our wedding day. I was embarking on a new journey with someone who loved me and was capable of taking care of me, and would lead me into a life of adventure and opportunity. For our honeymoon, I sold my car to pay for a three-week trip to Sri Lanka and the Maldives. It was a fantastic holiday, though the Maldives wasn't the luxurious destination it is today. Back then it was very basic, with accommodation little more than grass huts with corrugated roofs and regular power cuts. Nevertheless, we had a wonderful time. Unfortunately, I got mauled by the local mosquito population and returned home covered in bites. I had 75 bites down one arm alone! In fact, I felt so rough in the weeks after the honeymoon, I went to the doctor, who thought I may have picked up a tropical disease from the bites. But all the tests came back negative. Finally, he asked: 'Do you think you might be pregnant?'

'I don't think so…' I replied but took a test all the same. Sure enough, it was positive! That came as a shock to us both. Though we wanted children we hadn't planned on starting a family quite so soon. Nevertheless, our daughter Hannah arrived that May, 1987, just six weeks old at our first wedding anniversary.

In the months leading up to the birth, I reconnected with Mum and she offered to come and help out just after Hannah was born. But my mother never travelled light and she arrived at our house with several suitcases of clothes and accessories, most of which ended up lying around all over the house. She was soon bored with helping to look after me and the baby and demanded entertainment. When she did try to help she would cook extravagant meals that meant using all the pots and pans, leaving me to clear up the mess. In fact, it was a real relief when she left after two weeks as suspected – she'd been more trouble than the newborn baby!

I went back to work a few months after Hannah was born but we quickly found the cost of childcare was as much as I was earning so I gave up work altogether and soon fell pregnant again – this time with our son Aaron. I loved being a mother, giving my children the attention and affection they deserved, and always felt that I coped well. But after Aaron was born in June 1989, I was looking after a toddler and infant on my own all day while Raymond went off to work. I became increasingly lonely and overwhelmed.

One night Raymond was an hour late and by the time he walked in the door, I was absolutely furious. The sheer exhaustion of spending every second taking care of our baby and toddler and instead of coming straight home to relieve me, I became incensed to learn he'd spent an hour in the pub after work. *How thoughtless! How uncaring!* I told him I wasn't going to wash up the dirty dishes and he replied: 'Well, I don't do pots.' That made me so mad I took a hammer from the toolbox and smashed every single plate in the sink. Raymond was visibly shaken by my behaviour but at the time it felt damn good.

When I fell pregnant two years later I related this story to the health visitor and she said that my extreme reaction had likely been symptomatic of post-natal depression. So after our second son Jotham – Joe — was born in November 1991, the doctors gave me progesterone injections and a week of pessaries which worked to calm my hormones. I knew I had lost my cool that one time and I'd probably let things get on top of me. But generally I had no concerns about my mental health. And I never worried for a moment that I would be like my mother – our attitudes were polar opposite. While she put her own feelings at the centre of her world, my main concern was always for my children.

Those early years together seemed to pass quite quickly a blizzard of nappies, messy mealtimes and trips to the park. Raymond and I were ticking along quite nicely and he was doing well in his job as an insurance analyst. But when we moved to a bigger house in 1990 on The Wirral, Merseyside in the North West of England, things started to go wrong. The recession hit soon after our move and interest rates doubled overnight. We were on a terrible mortgage deal which tracked the Bank of England's base rate so our repayments shot up from three to 15 per cent. For the first time in our married lives, we were struggling.

'What are we going to do?' Raymond fretted as the bills piled up.

'Don't worry,' I reassured him. 'We'll be okay.' I'd grown up without money so our financial difficulties didn't bother me much. We had our kids, our health and happiness and I knew we could live with a few years of belt-tightening. But the circumstances grated on Raymond. He felt he wasn't providing properly for his family and when a new opportunity arose abroad, he believed that this was the chance we needed to make a better life for ourselves.

5

OUT OF THE DARKNESS

30 December 2007, South China Sea

'Right, we're not using the kettle anymore,' I told the rest of the crew on our second day at sea on the return journey to Hong Kong. It was in the middle of the afternoon that I was in the kitchen, making tea for the crew on watch, when the boat lurched to one side and I spilled boiling water down my foul weather gear.

'Shit!' I exclaimed as steaming water snaked down my waterproof jacket and trousers. Thank god I'd been wearing protective clothing or I could have been seriously hurt! It was a clear sign that it was time to dispense with the kettle and put the cooker off limits too. The going was too rough to risk having hot food flying around the galley.

'Okay, no one is to use the kettle or make hot food now,' I told the rest of the crew. 'We can all eat sandwiches and cereal until this weather clears.'

The going was now too rough and it wasn't worth the risk of someone getting burnt. Our trip back to Hong Kong had started out fairly smoothly. In fact, we had to use the engine to power out for the first 24 hours because there was no wind at all. We instituted the watch system right away and Victor quickly became part of the team, taking up his role with ease and efficiency. I was impressed by his speed and attention to detail and the way he didn't wait to be told what to do, he just did it. It was obvious that Victor had been sailing all his life, so he was a helpful crewmate to have on board. I began to see the wisdom of employing professional crew.

However, as we got further out to sea and lost sight of land, the wind began to build and we put up our sails. But we were cautious. We knew we were sailing into poor weather so we reefed our mainsail, ensuring we weren't under full power. Eventually we changed the foresail up to the storm jib, which is a smaller foresail, so we were under power of sail but not overpowered, and now the going became tedious. Along with the wind came the waves and the relentless bashing on the boat meant we were constantly bumping up and down. We were beating into the wind but not using the wind efficiently because we kept getting pushed back by the sea, so every time we hit a wave it slowed the boat. The chart plotter showed slower progress, the constant bashing of water on the bow pushing against our forward motion. It was frustrating but there wasn't much we could do about it. At this rate, we expected the trip to be a long slog back to Hong Kong, possibly a day longer than the five days as it was on the way over.

In fact, the return journey wasn't at all like the outbound one when it was sunny and warm enough to wear shorts and T-shirts on deck. With the wind and the cold, we all donned our foul weather gear to keep us dry and warm. I consoled myself with the thought that at least Hannah wasn't on board. She would have been horribly seasick with all this bumping up and down. Now we were heading home and, to be honest, I just wanted to get there. It wasn't much fun sailing in this weather. We had sailed in all weathers at weekends, but this had a different feel because there was no easy end to it, we couldn't just turn round and head back to the marina. We had to press on and adjust our sails and our minds to the current situation.

We knew rough weather was coming. Still, it didn't make for pleasant sailing and there was no more sunbathing or lolling around on deck, we just gritted our teeth and got on with it, adjusting our behaviour to fit the conditions. Tea and coffee were off the menu and we all lay in our bunks a lot longer when we weren't on watch, letting the bumps nod us off to sleep. Truth be told, the weather was tiring and though we were lucky that none of us got seasick we were all a little worn out by the relentless thumping up and down. We weren't expecting any change soon either, anticipating at least another two days of bumping along like this, making us all tired and uncomfortable. But they were just bumps, after all, and though not very fun, at least we weren't surfing up and down mountainous waves.

That night, I took my turn on watch with Victor and Raymond in the cockpit from 8pm till midnight. There were no stars or moon in the sky, it was pitch black on the sea and we could see nothing beyond what was lit up on the yacht surrounding us. Beyond the constant whacking of the boat against the waves there was no sound either. We talked little, each just focussing on our tasks, going about our jobs in quiet concentration. At 10pm, I was on the helm, Victor and Raymond were both in the cockpit. The watch system of four-hour shifts mandated us to maintain a group of three so we could take over the helm from each other and keep an eye on each other, making sure we were safe. The helming took concentration in these conditions so we didn't speak much, just the occasional comment about wind speed and compass reading.

Then, out of nowhere, a wall of water slammed into us and flooded the cockpit. I was thrown backwards and out onto the side deck. The tether attached to my lifejacket by a point at my chest snapped tight, like yanking a dog back on a leash, holding me fast to the boat. I lay sprawled on my back as Victor jumped up and grabbed the wheel. The boat juddered to a halt and the basket of equipment that normally sat at our feet in the cockpit swirled around in a pool of water, a few items falling over the side of the boat.

'What the hell was that?' I exclaimed. It was all over in a matter of minutes but it had come completely out of the blue.

'We must have hit a rogue wave,' said Victor, now gathering the remainder of our equipment back into the basket.

'Jesus, that was scary,' I breathed out, thankful at least for the 1.5 metre tether I was wearing.

The water quickly disappeared through the drain holes as I scrambled to my feet and hauled myself back into the cockpit, soaked through from head to toe. It took a moment for us to regroup, a moment of shock. Paul shouted up from below to see if we were okay.

'We hit a huge wave, but we're okay,' I shouted back. Then the boat picked up the familiar forward plod and the thumping into the waves began again.

We were all slightly in shock. If I hadn't been attached to the boat, I would have been swept overboard in the darkness. I was aware of rogue waves out at sea, caused by large ships or tankers passing miles away, creating massive waves in their wake. They were rare, freak occurrences but I'd never experienced one until now. It was extraordinary how it had engulfed the whole boat in a matter of seconds, leaving chaos and confusion in its wake. I was thankful at least that I hadn't seen it coming or I might have been terrified.

'How big do you think it was?' I asked the other two. I couldn't really judge the height of the wave because at the moment it was on us I was flying backwards out of the cockpit. It just felt like we had hit a giant concrete wall.

'Maybe 20, 30 feet,' said Raymond. 'I couldn't really tell either. I think it reached about halfway up the mast...'

'Yeah, about that,' agreed Victor. 'At least we hit it face on – it could have been worse.'

God, he was right! It struck me then that we had been lucky. Since we were beating into the weather, the wave had come towards us from the front. If it had hit us sideways it could have knocked the boat over. Then we would have been in real trouble.

We shone a light up the mast but the sails were still up and the boat was manoeuvring well so we assumed there hadn't been any permanent damage from the impact. Still, for the remainder of the watch we were all hyper vigilant, making our checks more regularly and carefully than before. The rogue wave had shaken us and though I knew it was unlikely we would encounter another one so soon after the first, it made me fearful of what else could be out there in the darkness. We made a quick inventory of our equipment and thankfully, apart from a pair of night vision goggles and a few bottles of water, the loss had been minimal.

At midnight, Martin, Aaron and Paul came on watch to relieve us and we filled them all in about the rogue wave. Now Raymond and I went down below, removing our foul weather gear, and hanging them on the hooks near the companionway, the raised hatchway which led down to the salon. But as I entered the lounge area, something caught my eye. I stared at the carbon fibre mast as it ran through the salon: *something didn't look right.* The mast was bolted onto the keel and ran from the ceiling down to the floor. It was designed this way to make it stronger, but in order to blend with the interiors, the part of the mast which ran through the salon was encased in a white padded covering.

Now, as I stood staring at it, I noticed that the covering had slightly shifted. It was only a very small change, probably imperceptible to anyone not familiar with the boat, but I could tell that the cover now was ruffled and slightly off centre where previously it lay flat against the mast. By now, I was so well-attuned to our boat and knew every part of her so well that even this tiny change was obvious to me the moment I set eyes on it.

'Look, Raymond,' I pointed to the covering. 'Do you think the mast is okay? That covering isn't straight anymore. It's off.'

'Hmmm…' he murmured, squinting at the cover. 'Yeah, maybe. Well, there's nothing much we can do about it now. Let's take a look at it in the morning.'

He was right. It was night and still pitch-black outside. Even if we found a problem, we couldn't fix it in the dark. I ran my hand over the covering, feeling the deep creases against my fingertips. *This has just happened*, I was sure, and it concerned me. *Tomorrow, I promised myself. Tomorrow, I'll undo the Velcro straps and check the mast underneath. It could just be the cover itself but if it's anything more serious we can get it looked at when we get back to Hong Kong.* I yawned deeply. It had been a long night and all I wanted was to lie down and get some rest.

I curled up in bed in the master cabin next to Raymond and closed my eyes, trying to put the dramatic events of the night behind me. But the adrenaline was still coursing through my body and though I wasn't hurt, I felt again the impact on my body as the wave forced me backwards. It was truly bizarre how quickly things could change at sea and how danger seemed to rear up out of nowhere without any warning. As I lay in bed, I recalled an incident the previous summer with Hannah and her friend Helen when Raymond and I had taken them on the yacht the day after a night of heavy partying. Both were hungover but convinced a refreshing trip on the water would blow out the cobwebs.

We had just started out and I was on the helm, navigating our way across the shipping lanes for a gentle sail from Aberdeen to Lamma Island. Although it was warm and sunny, the sea was choppy from a storm the day before and we were rocking more than usual. Raymond and Hannah nodded off in the cockpit but the waves weren't helping Helen's hangover and she was slumped over the small seat on the back deck, clinging to the rails, threatening to throw up over the side. Then, just as we crossed the shipping lanes under sail, the yacht heeled, catching Helen by surprise. She tumbled over the rails and into the sea. I didn't see it because I was in the cockpit, but I heard the scream. I looked back and saw Helen in the water. *Shit!* Thank god she was a good swimmer and not in any immediate danger of drowning but we were at the edge of a shipping lane and I could see there was a large ship approaching us. Time was of the essence. We sprang into action. I crash-stopped the yacht under sail by rounding her up into the wind and fired up the engine. We dumped the sails and Hannah threw a lifebuoy over to Helen. Now I turned the yacht round under engine power and approached slowly with lines for her to grab hold of and collect her from the sea.

Although every fibre in my body was telling me not to cross in the path of an oncoming vessel, we didn't have any choice. We had to retrieve Helen from the water. Thankfully, we carried it all out perfectly and with many meters to spare before the ship plodded past. But it felt like a close call. After that my nerves were shot to pieces and there was no question of carrying on our sailing trip for the day. We returned to the marina and back at home, I made myself a large cup of tea to recover my composure. Helen laughed it off as a foolish mistake but I don't think she realised just how much danger she had been in during those vital few minutes in the water. Situations can change in a split second at sea and then you have to know exactly what to do in order to keep your crew safe. It seemed the more we sailed, the

THE WATER RABBIT

more aware I was of everything that could go wrong.

The continuous bumping of the waves finally rocked me into a deep slumber but I was awoken at 4.00 a.m. when the watch changed over and Raymond got up to join Victor and Joe in the cockpit. After he left, I tried to doze off again but it was no good, I was wide awake and the dawn sunlight was beginning to creep into the cabin. By now, I was used to sleeping in four hours shifts at sea. I saw Martin was awake in the front cabin. He looked restless, like a man who had tried to sleep but failed.

'I wonder how much longer we'll have to put up with this...' he said. 'It's getting a bit tedious, this constant pounding into the waves.'

'I'm more concerned about the beating the boat is taking,' I said to Martin. 'And how long before something breaks?'

Incredibly, moments later, as if by speaking those very words I'd activated some unseen trigger we heard a loud CRACK. To my ears, it sounded like one of the sails breaking loose from its winch and I waited to hear the whipping of the sail as it flapped around in the wind. But we didn't hear that. Instead, everything went quiet. It felt like the boat had stopped moving. Martin and I looked at each other quizzically. Now Joe appeared at the entrance hatch and shouted down: 'We've lost the mast! All hands on deck, all hands on deck!'

6

A New Life

March 1994, Hong Kong

I DREW BACK the bedroom curtains to an incredible scene outside our window; the bluest of skies matched by a sapphire ocean and a yacht sailing gently past. A broad smile broke out over my face – this was utterly idyllic! The spacious apartment overlooked Repulse Bay, one of the most prestigious places in the south of Hong Kong Island, and we had landed here for a month, courtesy of Raymond's new company, while we searched for a place of our own. We had arrived by taxi the night before and now I was up early, keen to get an idea of our surroundings.

'Wow!' I breathed in wonder. It was simply the most stunning view I could imagine: calm, elegant and completely different to everything I had ever known. And there was the sea! My happiest childhood memories were the holidays taken in my grandparents' caravan by the sea to Hornsea or Scarborough, in Yorkshire, an escape from my difficult home life. And here it was again, an endless horizon of moving mass that formed and reformed constantly. A world of emergent, restless, permanent possibility, carrying with it all my hopes and dreams of a new beginning. At that moment a single thought crossed my mind: *We're going to make this work.* I just knew it. Hong Kong represented a new life for us, a new era and somehow, I felt it had

THE WATER RABBIT

always been my destiny.

I recalled an incident when I was just five years old, playing with a doll at the bottom of my Grandma's stairs. As I'd turned my doll over I noticed that she had a stamp on the back of her head with some words on it. At the time I was only just learning to read, so I tried to sound out the letters, just as I'd been taught in school.

'Mmmmm....ade.... in.... H....Hong... K...Kong...' I said aloud.

Hmm... that must mean it's made of something called 'Hong Kong', like a material.

'Oh, I thought it was plastic,' I exclaimed to myself in surprise.

Then a voice spoke to me: 'It's a place and you will go.'

Who said that? I looked around but there wasn't anybody there. *Hong Kong is a place? How do I get there?* I wondered. I didn't even know where it was. It was all very strange.

The following year, a new boy joined our class in primary school. This was quite an event in our small corner of Cheshire – it was rare for anybody to leave or for new people to arrive. So I paid very close attention when our teacher Mr Delaney made the announcement that 'Nicholas' was starting the following day.

'...and he's come all the way from Hong Kong,' he added at the end. 'So we must make him very welcome.'

Hong Kong! Just like my doll!

I remembered the stamp on my doll's head and I started to grasp the idea that Hong Kong was a real place. These were the days long before the internet when information was hard to come by; if you didn't see it on TV or read about it in a book there was little way of gaining knowledge about faraway places. I'd never come across China or Hong Kong before – we didn't even have a Chinese restaurant near us – so I was fascinated when this blonde-haired boy arrived the next day, all the way from an exotic, distant-sounding place.

As Nicholas ran around the playground, I plucked up the courage to approach him.

'Where's Hong Kong?' I asked curiously. 'And why are you here in Cheshire?'

'My dad is the head of the police force,' he replied.

'Oh, where is he the head of the police force?'

'In Hong Kong!'

'So it's a place then?'

Nicolas looked at me as if I was stupid, then ran off. I stood there, feeling foolish but at least it was confirmed: Hong Kong was real, just like the mysterious voice had said. Now, oddly, twenty-five years later, I was about to embark on a new life here.

For ten years, we had lived on The Wirral while Raymond built his career as an insurance analyst. The three kids had all arrived at two-year intervals and things were going well until the recession hit in the early nineties and we were locked into a mortgage deal that tracked the interest rate, crippling us financially. Hannah had been at private school but we could no longer afford the fees so we rented out our house and moved down to Milton Keynes, near to Mum, where there was a very good state school. I tried to make a real effort with Mum as she clearly adored her three grandkids. She was still annoyed, but I was keen my kids would have some access to grandparents between my Mum and Dad at least. We took the lease on a tiny house on an estate and now Raymond commuted by train every day to either the London or Liverpool office of his company. This was temporary, we agreed; we would live here for eighteen months at most, in the hope that the recession would be over by then and we could move back home.

At first Raymond had worked as an actuary at an insurance company but realising he was not valued there – he was overlooked for promotion — he applied for a job as an analyst at a merchant bank in Liverpool. But they felt he lacked a stockbroking background so Raymond approached his own stockbroker. They offered him a position and ironically, he started work on Black Monday — the name commonly attached to the global, sudden, severe, and largely unexpected stock market crash on October 19, 1987 which was of course terrible, but darkly humorous. 'Are you sure you didn't press the wrong button, Raymond?' my dad had teased.

After a year of learning the ropes and impressing the partners there, the merchant bank he had originally applied to sought him out. Now, working in Liverpool with frequent trips to London, Raymond soon became an excellent insurance analyst. He was clearly very smart and made excellent predictions about projected profits in the City, securing a good deal of money for the bank. But again, he was undervalued by his employers and with the recession starting to bite, he began scouting for opportunities. To my mind, we could battle through the lean times. After all, I had grown up with very little and though money was tight, it wasn't the end of the world. But Raymond felt frustrated and vented this frustration often.

One night I was alone at home since Raymond was staying over in Liverpool. I was watching the news when an item appeared about a new airport being built in Hong Kong. I thought back to our previous trip to this city the year before we married and remembered how unfriendly it felt due to the difficult family circumstances. But now I had a sense it would play a role in our future. And at that exact moment the phone rang — a man asking for Raymond. I explained he would not be back until the next day. He didn't wish to leave a message but I found out later, from Raymond, he was a headhunter, offering Raymond the chance to be a bank analyst in Hong Kong. It was incredible timing and to me, the proposal made perfect sense; Raymond's talents were not being fully utilised and felt sure that Hong Kong offered the opportunities to match his intelligence and ambition. So after some deliberation, we decided to take a chance and relocate to Hong Kong. There was just one issue – Mum. She wasn't at all happy about our move.

After a year of living in the same town Mum had become accustomed to the idea of seeing her grandchildren regularly and took it as a personal slight when we told her we were planning on taking them to another country. Our relationship had never been easy and in the run up to Joe's birth she had said some horrible things, accusing me of being 'unstable' and insisting I should get an abortion because she thought I couldn't cope. This was rich coming from a mother who had walked out on her own children! But we had managed to move past that row since, like with so much of her behaviour, I chose to forget her hurtful words for the sake of peace. I wanted so much for us to have at least one Grandma in the kids' lives, and Hannah adored her Paw Paw (Cantonese for maternal Grandma). So I forgave Mum and everything settled down again.

When we moved to Milton Keynes we got into a routine where I would take the kids round to her place once a week and cook dinner for the whole family in an effort to bring us all together. By now she was married for a third time and her new husband, Alan, was a down-to-earth man. He'd sadly lost his first wife to suicide and he was a very loyal husband to my mother. The kids liked him as he was fun and playful and I liked him too. He was very kind and helpful and pretty handy at DIY so he occasionally helped with small jobs around the house. Just before our move to Hong Kong in March 1994, we gave up the lease on the small house and moved in with them both for the last remaining month in the UK. We had already sold our house on The Wirral to pay off all our bills and shipped out most of our furniture. Now we were just waiting for Raymond to work out his notice.

On reflection now, I can see moving in with her for the last six weeks were in the UK, especially given her past outbursts was always going to be testing, but she had offered and I thought it would be nice for the children to spend time with her before we left. But the longer we were there, the more fuss she made about our upcoming relocation. She said it was the wrong decision for all sorts of reasons and, like a toddler having a tantrum, she insisted she simply wouldn't tolerate it.

'You're not taking my grandchildren out of the country,' she announced imperiously over and over again. 'You're just not doing it.'

'Mum, it's not your choice,' I'd reply as calmly as I could. 'I know that we can try for a better life there. The recession here is killing Raymond's job, he's not going to go anywhere with it. We'll visit, I promise, and you can come out to see us as often as you like…'

But nothing I said placated her and the closer it got to our departure date, the more difficult she became.

Four days before we were due to leave, I was in the kitchen preparing dinner when she walked in shouting: 'You shouldn't go to Hong Kong. It's a shit hole!' It was just one of her usual outbursts that seemed to flare up with no provocation.

'But, Mum, you've never been to Hong Kong. You don't *know* that,' I countered.

I was getting sick of this, her attacking my decisions, once again hurling insults to get her own way. I just wasn't in the mood for it. I'd had a full day of looking after three kids and I was trying to cook dinner for everyone. *God, it's hot in here!* I removed my jumper. Mum kept the central heating cranked up to the highest setting so we were all roasting in March. Joe was toddling around in a nappy and t-shirt, Hannah had on her school uniform and Aaron was in his *Thunderbirds* outfit. I was hot, sweaty and annoyed with her. What I needed now was help, a bit of support, not this constant barrage of attacks and insults!

'Nothing will end well if you go there,' she went on. 'Raymond will become really Chinese again if you go back to Hong Kong and you'll be on your own. You're being stupid. You're making the biggest mistake of your life, Carolyn. Mark my words...'

Something took control of me. I felt something break inside of me as if I was a different person. I turned on her.

'Will you just shut up? Just shut up!' I begged.

'Why don't you take your witch act somewhere else?' she screamed back, then stormed upstairs and into her bedroom.

I've had enough of this shit! I couldn't stop myself, a rage came over me. I had enough pressure sorting the move. I threw the pan in the sink and raced up the stairs after her. As soon as I appeared at her bedroom door she started bawling at me again as my own red mist descended. Thirty years of my mother's selfish behaviour bubbled to the surface... thirty years of dealing with her insults, her abuse, her neglect, her disregard for me, my choices and my feelings. It all bubbled to surface and in that moment I wanted to kill her. I put my hands around her throat and I started to squeeze, screaming: 'I HATE YOU! YOU'VE NEVER BEEN A GOOD MOTHER TO ME. NEVER. NEVER. I'M GOING TO GO TO HONG KONG AND I'M TAKING MY KIDS WITH ME.'

I could have killed her. I really could have. It is the only time in my life I have ever felt that rage. Her face went red. She didn't say anything. I saw she was crying and I stopped. I experienced a moment of clarity and my hands went limp. I let go, took a step backwards and knew that the only sane thing I could do at that moment was leave. *I have to get out of here. I have to leave the house.*

I ran downstairs, grabbed the kids in their flimsy clothes and bundled them out of the house and into the freezing March night. We drove to Milton Keynes station where I waited for Raymond to arrive, breathing hard, still in shock at everything that had just happened. Raymond saw us and knew something was wrong the moment he clocked the three kids in the car.

'What's going on?' he asked, looking at the children shivering in the backseat.

'I'm never going back to that house,' I said shakily.

'Why? What's happened?'

'I'm not going back and the kids are not going back either,' I repeated, eyes fixed straight ahead, knuckles white from gripping the steering wheel.

'Right. Let's go and figure this out.'

We drove to McDonald's for dinner and while the kids ran around the play area I filled Raymond in on everything that had happened that evening. I told him how I was over all the drama Mum brought into my life. How she tried to ruin everything that didn't serve her own needs. Raymond was calm, he was not totally surprised as tensions had been rising steadily ever since the Hong Kong decision was made. He agreed the kids were not to go back to her house. We needed a plan. We called my brother and arranged to stay with him just outside Milton Keynes for the last three nights before our flight. We took the kids to my brothers and left them there.

'Right, all we need to do now is collect our things from the house and return the keys,' Raymond said.

'No, I don't want to go back,' I said, sick at the thought of seeing her again.

'We have to — all our clothes are there,' he said. 'Look, it will be fine. I'll make sure nothing happens, we'll just grab our things and leave.'

Later that same night, we drove back and as we pulled up outside the house, my stomach turned over with nervous anticipation. Inside, I could hear raised voices. Now Raymond looked at me, and nodded firmly, a look that said: *Don't worry, we'll face this together*.

Inside the house, Mum was hysterical and Alan was now there too, also visibly upset. Raymond did his best to calm the situation down. He went into the room where Mum and Alan were sitting and tried to reason with her that the move was for the best, a better future for us and the kids. Raymond ordered me to go upstairs and start packing our belongings.

I didn't say a word. I just raced up the stairs and flew around, throwing everything I could find into our suitcases. Downstairs, I heard my mother weeping and wailing, but I couldn't hear the words and I tried to block it out anyway. I grabbed anything I could see that was ours. There was no folding or careful placing of items, I just bundled armfuls of our belongings into bags. Then, just as I was getting the last of our things, she came up the stairs behind me, grabbed me by the hair and dragged me out of the bedroom, calling me names. Telling me I wouldn't cope, I was a useless mother, I was cruel and selfish. She picked up a framed wedding photo of me and Raymond and chucked it at my head. It narrowly missed me, smashing against the wall, shattering everywhere. Raymond bounded up the stairs after her, ushered her out of the room and shouted at me: 'Keep packing!' while he transferred the bags to the car. The whole thing took about twenty minutes and after we got everything in the back of the car, we handed the front door key back to Alan, who was crying on the doorstep, in shock, speechless.

I said: 'I'm very sorry.' I turned and I left. I never spoke to my mother again after that night. After years of trying to appease her, forgive her, keep the peace and stay sane at the same time, the relationship was over. She had seen to that. I regretted losing my temper and putting my hands on her but at the time I was overcome with a rage I'd never felt before or since. It wasn't me. I didn't recognise myself. She had pushed and pushed until I'd snapped. I never wanted to feel that rage again, that complete loss of control. I knew I had to cut her out of my life for good, for my health, my sanity and my safety.

Four days later, Raymond enjoyed his farewell drinks at work and came straight to the airport for our flight. We had the kids, thirteen pieces of luggage and my dad with us. He had been laid off a year earlier and we asked him to join us in Hong Kong for the first year, while he rented out his home. As we got on the plane that day, I knew I had everything I wanted with me right there. I would never rebuild my relationship with my mother again after what had happened. She was just too selfish and toxic to let back into my life. Raymond had tried to keep in touch with his dad as much as he could, but over the years it got more difficult because his dad's health started to fail and his mother was his carer. If Raymond rang up to talk to his Dad she complained so much that, in the end, it wasn't worth it and the calls stopped. Chinese friends said my mother-in-law would come round after I had my first child – but she didn't. And then they predicted she would relent when I had my first son, but no. It was a shame as I really could have done with the help of a Grandma, especially since she only lived two miles down the road! I even imagined our children would grow up bilingual if they spoke Chinese with his family, but they were never given that opportunity. I felt sorry for Raymond particularly. He was very loyal to his family and before he met me, he'd been close to his mum. It was a sad loss to all of us and I felt somewhat guilty that he'd had to make that choice to be with me.

There was very little I wanted in England and some small part of me knew that this move had always been written into my life's journey. Those words came back to me now: 'It's a place and you will go.' We'd thrown our whole future into this move. After selling the house and paying off our bills, we boarded the plane with just £3,000 in the bank. That was it. We had nothing else. If it all went wrong and we had to fly back, the money would pay for our air tickets and nothing else. There wouldn't be a penny left. Raymond and I both knew the significance of this moment and each of us silently contemplated the way ahead as we travelled through the night to Hong Kong.

At some point during the flight, while we soared over the Middle East and the kids slept soundly beside me, Raymond leaned in and whispered: 'You know, I've no idea what a banking analyst does.'

A moment of self-doubt, a flicker of uncertainty in a man otherwise brimming with confidence.

'This is not a job I know...' he went on.

'You'll be fine,' I reassured him. 'Every job you've gone to you've made a difference and this will be no exception. You're so smart, Raymond. Honestly, you're going to be fine. I know it.'

It was true. I never doubted Raymond for a moment. I knew that with the right opportunities there was no limit to his ambition. Whatever challenges he faced, he would rise to meet them.

Landing at the famous old Kai Tak airport in Hong Kong was a thrilling experience. We descended through brightly lit housing estates on either side and for a brief moment it was as if the tips of the wings would collect the laundry that was hanging outside people's apartment windows. Then we touched down and came to a screeching halt before the end of the runway terminated at the very edge of the harbour. We took a taxi to the apartment which Raymond's company had provided for us. They had originally offered to pay for a hotel but Raymond insisted we needed the amenities of an apartment in order to look after the kids properly. Thankfully, the apartment they found was large and luxurious and would have been out of our own price range, but it was perfect for our first month. The next morning, I pulled back the curtains on the idyllic view of Repulse Bay. *What a view! Well, winter in the UK can get stuffed! This is our new life now and we are going to make it work.*

We stayed in Repulse Bay for a month before signing a lease on an apartment in a more family-friendly outlying island where rents were cheaper than Hong Kong Island. The apartment there was big enough for my dad to have his own room and there was space for the kids to play outdoors. Also, the area was populated by lots of expats so it felt there was less of an adjustment for us. A few of Raymond's old university friends also lived in Hong Kong and during our first fortnight there, one family invited us to dinner. It was evening when we arrived and I could tell from the large house, these people were very wealthy. They had a couple of children of their own, who were running wild all over the house, as three harassed-looking domestic helpers chased round after them. I was quite bemused by all this mayhem, particularly the fretful-looking staff who had more than their hands full. The mother, however, seemed totally unconcerned as she invited us through to the lounge for a drink.

'Where's *your* maid?' she enquired, as my own three children sat quietly by my side.

'I don't have one,' I replied.

'Oh, you *must* have a maid!' she exclaimed. 'Then you can do so much more with your time.'

I wasn't convinced. *Why would I need a maid? I've done everything myself for six years now and never had any help in all that time. Besides, even with three helpers this family were in chaos!*

But that night, coincidentally on our way home, Raymond said: 'We have to get a maid.'

'Why?'

'When we want to go out, the maid can look after the kids.'

'But my dad's here...'

'No, there's the cleaning, washing and cooking. She can do all that for us.'

So I relented and we employed a lovely woman called Marina to take on the domestic chores. And now that Marina was doing all the housework I decided to get a job in an office to help me to learn Cantonese and acclimatise better. I also joined a tennis club to meet new friends and build up my social life.

However, Hong Kong is a transient place and at first, I was thrown together with people who weren't quite my cup of tea, wives of British contractors on two-year contracts who talked about leaving the moment they arrived. These women spent all their time complaining and it got on my nerves.

'Oh, I miss my four bedroom house and my garden in Gloucester,' they moaned. 'We're all cramped together in a small apartment out here with just a tiny balcony.'

Tsk. Hong Kong isn't that bad, I thought as they whined about all the things they missed about England. *You've been given an incredible opportunity to see another country and all you can do is bitch about it!* The experience was wasted on them. Fortunately, I also met some really nice, down-to-earth people in those early years and we remain friends to this day. From the moment we arrived, I knew we were here to stay. That meant putting down solid roots and surrounding myself with good people, people who appreciated the opportunities of living in a new country. I'd learned from many years of dealing with my mother that there was little to be gained from negative-thinking. I didn't see the

THE WATER RABBIT

point in wasting each day complaining. Besides, my dad was with me and I couldn't have been happier to be away from my mum.

7

Pan Pan

'All hands on deck!'

On hearing those words from Joe we all jumped off our beds, grabbed our foul weather gear and ran up on deck to find out what was happening.

Oh my god! I couldn't believe it when I saw the whole length of the mast lying across the yacht and jutting out into the water. From there, it seemed to have snapped again, bending over the side of the boat into an L-shape so that the end of the mast pointed downwards, disappearing into the water. What on earth had happened? The carbon fibre seemed to have exploded, splintering into tiny pieces just above the roof of the cabin. Nothing was left upright. Nothing! Worse, it had dragged all the sails with it and now the boat was leaning port side, making us list. Now we were rolling around in the waves and it was clear we had to cut loose all the sail immediately because we were unstable. If we had any chance of getting the yacht back to shore we had to use the engine and with all those lines dragging in the water, we couldn't do a thing. We had to act fast.

Raymond asked Martin to go to the bow and remove the split pin that was still attached at the base of the forestay. We donned our lifejackets and the crew got to work cutting away all the stays and the rigging, tethered onboard of course. It was clear that nothing was salvageable.

THE WATER RABBIT

'I think we should all take a seasickness pill,' I said. 'The last thing we need is for anyone to get ill right now.'

I went below and found the pills. Although I never usually get seasick, we were now at the mercy of the waves, slopping around in the ocean, and there was every chance it would make one of us queasy. The weather now was quite poor and we were rocking heavily. As soon as we were free of all the mast and rigging we could turn the engine on and start making headway again. Then at least we wouldn't be left bobbing around like a cork. But where to head to?

I went below to use the satellite phone. The first person I called was our friend Simon, who had sold us all our safety equipment and was one of the most experienced sailors I knew.

'We've lost the rig,' I told him. 'The mast shattered and we couldn't save a thing.'

I gave him our position and asked for his advice.

'Let me check the charts and call you back,' he said.

It took an hour to cut all the mast and rigging away – even with the hydraulic bolt cutters – and then we heaved everything into the ocean. Now the boat had no mast, no sails and we were at the mercy of the motion of the waves. We were still afloat and had power, but being so far from land — about 300 nautical miles — and having lost our main means of propulsion was alarming. However, we did have our engine still so we put that on and tried to make headway towards our destination. We weren't making good progress – just 5 knots – but we had to do something. We couldn't sit in the sea and at least, with some motion, we felt a bit more stable and in control than if we were simply sitting there. It wasn't long before Simon called back.

'Don't head any further towards Hong Kong,' he instructed. 'You're around 400 miles from us but the weather is getting worse here, worse than what was predicted, so there's no point heading into it. Turn around and if you can stay on the boat, head back towards the Philippines, away from the weather.'

So we turned the boat around and headed back towards the Philippines, which was around half the distance from Hong Kong. But by now the sea was quite rough and we were no longer in harmony with it, we were just a vessel, bouncing around, making very little headway. You can manoeuvre a yacht under sail, going with the weather, but without a mast or sails we were just a vessel, stricken in these waves. And worse, we were taking on water.

We could hear the bilge pump working continuously on automatic, which meant there was water coming in somewhere. But where? It was vital we found the hole as quickly as possible. So we started lifting up the floorboards and seats in the cabin to have a look at the condition of the hull underneath. We had the equipment necessary to repair the damage: wooden bungs to hammer in, as well as sticky patches. The only problem was, we couldn't find the hole. Raymond and I went searching all around the cabin, ripping the cushions off all the seats, lifting every floorboard and examining every inch of the bottom of the boat with our torches. Though we could both see the water building beneath us in the hull, neither of us could spot any obvious damage.

We assumed one of the spreaders had cracked the hull. On a mast there are long spikes a couple of feet long that stick out to support the mast. It seemed most likely that one of these spreaders had pierced the hull when the mast went over, but we had no idea where that was. And now we were in real trouble. Water was coming in, we couldn't find the hole to stop it so things weren't going to get any better. The bilge pump was tolerating it for the time being but we didn't know for how long. It was no good – we needed help. At around 7.00 a.m. I put out a Pan

Pan distress call on the radio. The Pan Pan message meant we were in trouble and in urgent need of assistance, but there was no imminent danger to life, unlike with a May Day call.

The first people I spoke to were at the Maritime Rescue Coordination Centre (MRCC) in Hong Kong. I gave them our coordinates and explained the situation.

'I don't think things are going to get any better,' I told them. 'It looks like we're going to need to be rescued. What can you do to help? Can you send a helicopter?'

'Hmm... it looks like you're too far for a helicopter to come out. We can only send a helicopter if it can land on the oil rigs 100 miles offshore to refuel,' explained the duty controller.

'But the weather in Hong Kong is bad and we don't know if the helicopter can refuel in these conditions. If it can't refuel it won't be able to reach you. But, look, we will confirm with the pilot and call you back.'

I sat and waited by the satellite phone. In the meantime, the emergency channel crackled to life as a ship responded to my Pan Pan distress call.

'We are in the area,' the captain said. 'What sort of vessel are you and what help do you need?'

'We are a 50-foot pleasure yacht – we've lost our mast, we're taking on water and we're unlikely to make it back to shore. We are a crew of seven in need of rescue.'

There was a pause on the other end of the line.

'I'm really sorry but we can't do it,' he said eventually. 'We're too big to help you. We're a large vessel, you're a small yacht and it's just not going to work. We can't rescue you but we will relay a message of help.' I was dismayed. Maybe the helicopter couldn't reach us either. We would definitely need some help, but for now, we would keep going as long as we could. I felt calm at this stage. My training had kicked in and I was clear what I needed to do, putting into practice everything I had learned in my courses. Besides, panic would have been a waste of precious energy. Nothing was going to happen quickly and in the very worst case scenario, we could deploy the life raft, but we were a long way from that at this stage.

A few minutes later, the MRCC duty controller called back.

'We've spoken to the pilot and he says they can't land on the oil rigs so we can't send a helicopter,' he said. 'But we can send a spotter plane.'

'What will that do?'

'Well, it will circle your position to locate you and drop green dye on the surface of the sea for easier location. In the meantime, we'll see who else is in the area to help you.'

Now it was 7.30 a.m. and our situation was rapidly deteriorating. The storm was building around us and water was steadily filling up the hull. Things could only get worse from this point, it was just a matter of how quickly that would happen.

That's when we received a call from the captain of the *Maersk Princess*, an oil tanker en route from Taiwan to Thailand. Captain Sirpreet Khalon said they were in the area and could assist but they had to turn around first and that would take two hours.

'In the meantime, what is your status?' he said. 'I can put together a plan, but please be aware, this rescue isn't negotiable. I am the captain, I am in control. If I rescue you, you have to do exactly as I say. We will bring the ship relatively close to you – as close to you as possible on the windward side, that way you will be in the shadow of the tanker, sheltered from the wind and the water. From there I'll let you know what we are going to do.'

Thank God! It was a great relief to know that help was on its way. Yes, we were adrift 200 miles from land but at least we weren't alone. Now, at 8.30 a.m. and with the ship turning around to get us, I called Hannah who was back home in Hong Kong. It had been three hours since we had lost the mast but I hadn't wanted to contact her until there was a rescue plan in place.

'Hannah, it's me. Look, we've got a situation here,' I started. 'We've lost the mast...'

'Oh shit!' She knew immediately what this meant.

'... yes, but look, it's okay. We've got a tanker coming round to get us. It will probably be here in two hours. It's going to pick us up and take us on board. I'll call you and update you when we're all on board. It does mean that once we are on the tanker we will have to go with it to Thailand.'

'Okay,' she said. 'It sounds serious, but you seem to have it under control. I love you. Stay safe.'

Next, I rang my sailing friend Andy to let him know the situation.

'Will you please also ring my best friend Reine and ask to go round and sit with Hannah for the day?' I asked. 'I don't want her to be on her own, wondering what the hell is going on. Please, just ask Reine to be there for her.'

Andy agreed. Now at least I knew my daughter had the company of an adult, somebody who she could turn to for comfort and support, whatever the outcome. I didn't like to think of the possibilities — my mind simply wouldn't allow it — but I had to ensure that whatever happened, my daughter wasn't alone.

Things started to further deteriorate on the boat. The inverter — which takes power from the battery and converts it to the electricity for our sockets – started to smoke because of the ingress of water. So we had to shut it down, which turned off the electrics on our boat. There was no doubt about it – we had to be rescued.

By 9.00 a.m., we were all assembled in the cockpit, awaiting rescue, each of us concerned but calm. We could easily stay on board for another two hours, there was no immediate danger of the boat sinking and though the waves were now pretty big, everyone was safely inside the cockpit. It was now too dangerous to go below because the boat was moving and things were flying around. But I ventured down and quickly grabbed a box of Sugar Puffs and some milk and made everyone eat a bowl of cereal. None of us were hungry, of course, but we needed our energy for whatever lay ahead. Whilst in the galley, I looked around at the strewn cushions and lifted floorboards. Everything was in disarray. I grabbed hold of the cherry wood handrail to steady myself. The wood was so rich in colour and silky smooth. What a beautiful yacht she is! What a shame. A moment of sadness swept over me as I realised she was now heading for the bottom of the sea. But when – hours, days? I had no idea. All I knew was that *Purple X* would not be our haven for much longer.

Returning to the cockpit, I felt at least that we were safe until rescue arrived. We all had our lifejackets on and if the boat began to sink rapidly we also had our life raft. However, the saying goes: 'You don't step *down* into a life raft, you step *up* into it.' In other words, it is safest to stay on your vessel for as long as possible, while it is still above water. You only get into a life raft when one foot is already in the water and you have to step *up* to get in. We'd all heard apocryphal tales of crews abandoning ship and being lost to the waves in a flimsy life raft when months later, their vessel washes up on shore, still perfectly seaworthy. Indeed, weeks later, when we relayed details of our disaster to the Hong Kong Yacht Club, we encountered criticism from some members that we had '…stepped off a perfectly good boat'. That simply wasn't true. At this very moment, our boat was sinking at sea with two of our children on board. Rescue was our only option.

By around 11am, for the next two hours, my eyes were fixed

on the horizon, willing the *Maersk* tanker to appear. Nobody spoke much. It was strange, really, because we all knew the situation was precarious and perhaps we each played out the different scenarios silently in our minds, but we didn't give voice to our worries. Words seemed a waste of energy, besides we didn't have any. It seemed more appropriate to stay quiet. What could we say that wouldn't spark a barrage of questions or fears? Captain Sirpreet had issued his rescue plan over the satellite phone and now we needed to follow that procedure. At least a professional sea captain was now in charge of the next steps and this alleviated the stress a little.

After about an hour, the spotter plane appeared. The small aircraft circled the yacht, dropping lime green dye in the waters around us to highlight our location for the benefit of the *Maersk*. We saw the pilot wave to us out his window and we waved back. Given that we had no idea how long it would take for the *Maersk* to arrive and we had no idea how long the highlighter dye would last in the churning sea, his actions seemed a little pointless. Nevertheless, it was reassuring to see another human being at our time of distress, and we hoped that the ship would not be far behind. Finally, from a long way off we could make out the distinct long, thin silhouette of the ship emerging from the edge of the skyline.

'It's here,' I said to the others.

Even though we could see the tanker clearly, we couldn't be sure he could see us from the distance, so we let off our rocket flares to indicate our location. By now conditions were making visibility problematic — the water was grey, the sky was grey, the water had white caps on it and our tiny yacht was white so we blended in with the froth off the top of the waves.

We set off everything we had, launching our orange rocket flares skywards, one after another. And when they were done we lit the bright orange handheld flares and waved them around, sending plumes of thick orange smoke above our heads. Eventually, the *Maersk* started moving towards us, which meant that they had found our position. It was at this point I felt a surge of panic. Normally, in a sailing boat, you do everything you can to avoid oil tankers. These ships have absolute right of way and for one very good reason: they are huge and they can't stop easily. Now, seeing this 110,000-tonnes, 250-metre long megalith bearing down on us, I was overcome by dread. *It's too big. How on earth were we going to get off our yacht and onto that giant tanker?*

'Oh my god... Oh my God... Oh my god...' I muttered. I couldn't help it, the words just tumbled out of my mouth. My heart was racing, my stomach-churning. I felt sick with terror.

'Carolyn, shut up!' Raymond turned to me sternly. He was right – I had to keep it together, I couldn't afford to fall apart now. I had to be ready for whatever the next few hours had in store.

8

DAD

January 15 2000, Hong Kong

The call took me completely by surprise.

'Dad's had a stroke,' said my sister from her home in Peterborough. 'We found him lying in his hall at home. He'd been there a couple of days. He's in hospital now and he's recovering but he's paralysed down his left side. He'll be okay with a lot of rehabilitation.'

I could hardly believe it – my dad was only 61. Two summers ago, we had enjoyed an amazing road trip around Scotland together with the kids. It was only when I saw him at his home last year that I felt he seemed a little more fragile than before; perhaps it was his diabetes, maybe age was catching up with him, but it wasn't anything serious and when we hugged and said our goodbyes in August, I was already planning our next trip.

Dad had returned to the UK in 1995 after a year of living in Hong Kong with us. Though he had enjoyed his time here, he said he felt he was impinging on our family life. He also missed the UK and my sister Elizabeth was having her first baby, a little girl, and he wanted to be there for her arrival. The hot weather was also rather debilitating and he hid from the sun as much as he hid from the torrential rain. My sister now worked as a full-time teacher, as did her husband Simon, and Dad went round to their house once a week for Sunday lunch. He seemed to live a pleasant, quiet life — he had a small circle of friends and played bridge every week. But when his bridge partner went round to collect him for their usual game after the New Year, Dad failed to come to the door. His friend assumed he must have gone out and put a note through the door. When my sister rang him the next day and the call went straight to answer machine, she also assumed he'd popped out. But when he still wasn't picking up the following day she started to worry and sent Simon round to check on him. There was no answer at the door so Simon let himself in with his key and found Dad lying up the hall in a bad way. An ambulance was called and he was rushed to hospital.

'I need to come back and see him,' I said hurriedly.

'I'm not sure that's a good idea right now,' said Elizabeth. 'Honestly, Carolyn, if you come running back he'll think he's going to die. And he's not going to die. He's just going to need a lot of therapy.' She said that the stroke was serious, the blood clot was the size of a satsuma. Elizabeth said he'd slipped off a ladder six months earlier whilst trying to fix something on the outside of the house. It had left him bruised, shaken and with two unsightly black eyes so we knew he had hit his head in the fall. Had this caused the stroke?

'Perhaps you should wait till Easter when you've got holiday time. By then he'll be out of hospital, we'll have put in the adjustments to his house and he'll be a lot better.'

Until this moment I had never regretted our move to Hong Kong but right now it was torturous to be so far away from my dad. All I wanted was to see and speak to him. After I put the phone down to Elizabeth, I called the hospital and when I was put through to the ward, the staff wheeled the telephone to his bedside.

THE WATER RABBIT

'How you doing, Dad?' I asked gently.

He started sobbing. That caught me off-guard. Dad wasn't an emotional person and it was rare to hear him cry. But I'd heard that strokes can sometimes bring about changes to personality and behaviour.

'Come on, Dad,' I urged. 'It's not that bad.'

Still, he kept crying.

'Now look,' I tried to sound light-hearted. 'If you're just going to cry down the phone, I'll ring you back tomorrow!'

A couple of big sniffs, he was trying to pull himself together.

'You okay, Dad?'

'Yeah, yeah... sorry...' he said shakily.

'That's okay... I want to see you. Shall I come back? Shall I come and see you?'

'No. No, it's okay.'

'Are you sure? I can get on a plane tomorrow and I can come back.'

'No, don't do that. I'll be alright.'

We talked a little longer. Not much though, Dad seemed very tired. After I put the phone down, I thought hard about what to do. Although it had been good to hear his voice, I was upset at hearing him cry. But he seemed resolute.

'He doesn't want me to come back,' I told my sister when we spoke again. 'And judging from our conversation, I think you're probably right. He's very emotional at the moment and it will just disturb him more. He'll think the worst. Just keep me informed how it's going and I'll make plans to come back at Easter.'

By now we had been in Hong Kong nearly six years and it's fair to say our lives had changed considerably. At first, I had worked in an office where nobody spoke English so my Cantonese became quite good, something which annoyed Raymond no end because now I could understand every word he said on the phone! After a couple of years I gave up work and started volunteering at the kids' school, running the Cub Scout pack. Then I trained as a teaching assistant and started working with special needs children at my kid's High School.

Raymond, meanwhile, threw himself into work. When we had arrived in Hong Kong the British were planning to hand the territory back to the Chinese — which took place in 1997. There was a lot of concern among the local community of what would happen when the Chinese took over. Many Hong Kong people had already been overseas for years and gained their foreign passports in Britain, Canada and Australia. Now they returned, bringing a new perspective to Hong Kong but retaining their cultural understanding and language ability. There was a low-level animosity from the locals who didn't have the option of leaving and resented those who did. Expats always had a chance to leave, of course, so there was a lot of talk of 'wait and see what happens'. There was also a considerable amount of racism directed at the local Cantonese population from the foreign community. I heard many Australians and Brits describing them 'thick and uncouth' and generally looked down on them. This was all expressed in our presence — but then they would turn to Raymond, as if they'd just remembered he was there, and exclaim: 'Oh, but we don't mean Raymond! We don't mean *you*, Raymond!' It was not new to me and especially Raymond to be faced with these micro aggressions and casual racism.

The issue for Raymond was that he didn't fall into the expat camp and he didn't fall in the local camp either. He had been brought up in the British public school system and his Cantonese was thirty years out of date. He was caught between two worlds, so in the end he directed all his energy and attention towards his work. Raymond felt he had something to prove - to the mother who had disowned him (he was aware that his success or otherwise would reach his family) and to all the people who had underestimated him over the years, not to mention those who had been racist towards him in the UK and in Hong Kong. He was out to show them all. And once that drive to succeed got hold of him, it was all-consuming.

He rose quickly in the world of investment banking. He was so good at his job that within a very short time he was making more money than I had ever imagined possible. Our lifestyle changed – we moved to a bigger house, we could now afford long-haul, five-star holidays and the things I might have previously dismissed as financially out of reach became possible. I could afford any clothes or furniture that took my fancy. I was able to buy packages of facials and pay a decent hairdresser for a great cut and colour. School fees were no longer an issue and all the kids were in excellent international schools. To me, money meant freedom – it meant I could afford to keep our home the way I wanted it, live the life I wanted and take a holiday whenever I needed it. We were no longer constrained by financial considerations and that was a very liberating feeling.

For Raymond, however, money meant something else. There were certain goals, symbols that he aimed for and which, for him, fulfilled his idea of a successful life. For one thing, he had always dreamed of owning a Porsche. Now, to own a Porsche back in the days of living on The Wirral seemed like a ridiculous idea. To my mind, only football stars owned luxury sports cars. But having a Porsche in Hong Kong was even more outrageous. For one thing, in Hong Kong you pay 100% tax on cars, instantly doubling the price of any car, let alone a very expensive sports car! On top of that you had to pay for a parking space which, because Hong Kong was so overcrowded, was the price of a small house. Besides, public transport was so effective nobody really needed a car. We had a sensible little Honda at the time for running the kids around which was, to my mind, perfect for our needs. But even that wasn't a necessity.

One day in 1998 we had a friend over for lunch. He lived quite a bit further out of town from us in the seaside village of Stanley so Raymond suggested we take him home in the car.

'We'll run you back, have a pint in the Smuggler's Inn and come back.'

So I went downstairs to bring the car round but when I got to the car park I was annoyed to see that somebody had parked in our space. This was a strict no-no in Hong Kong.

'Who the hell's parked this Porsche in our space?' I said, irritably.

At that moment, Raymond clicked the remote key and the car opened up. It was *his* car? I stood there, mouth open, staring at this brand new purple 911.

'Well, how do you like it?' asked Raymond. He let me drive while he squashed into the back and our friend Richard took the passenger seat and off we went to Stanley. They say you get what you pay for, and driving the Porsche really was a wonderful driving experience — it seemed glued to the road and handled so well. But I was still quite amazed at Raymond's actions.

He had bought a brand new Porsche for cash like it was nothing! That's how much he was now earning in investment banking. I was shocked, but I understood that for him this was something he felt he deserved. All those late nights, those long hours spent away from home, away from his family, had to have some compensation for Raymond. And this was it. Yet, a few weeks later, he said to me: 'You know, I thought it would mean something to me. I've wanted this for so long, to own a Porsche, but it wasn't really anything in the end.'

We kept the car, we liked it, but as with so many things in life, what Raymond thought would make him happy, hadn't quite turned out that way.

By the start of 2000, Raymond's work was all-consuming. It had become harder to find time to be together, either as a couple or as a family. I frequently found myself alone at dinner parties, or turning up to black tie events in full evening gown only to get a phone call at the last minute: 'I can't make it. Sorry. You're on a table with some of my top clients – don't let me down!' He was involved in so many projects, the workload was immense. And urgent matters would crop up in our downtime, with Raymond managing calls between time zones in the USA and China, calls that went on late into the night. At home, Raymond was often stressed and tired. I'd try to talk to him about things and he'd snap: 'Oh, just get to the point. Say it!'

A distance started to creep into our relationship because it felt to me like we didn't have good conversations. Raymond was either away, too busy to talk or on the phone. I recalled the days when we lived on The Wirral after the recession struck and I would lie in bed, thinking: *If we just had £100,000 all our problems would be solved. We could pay off the house and live comfortably.* Yet, now, £100,000 wasn't even a bonus for Raymond and he was more miserable than ever. He was driven, he always had something to prove. But whatever he was achieving, it was never enough.

On 30 January, two weeks after Dad's stroke, I was in bed when the phone rang. The screen on our digital phone read 'LONG DISTANCE' so I picked it up, still half asleep, and my sister's voice came on the line.

'Dad's dead,' she said in tearful distress.

What?

There was a clang on the other end of the line and sobbing in the background. It sounded like she had dropped the phone. *What the hell's going on? How could Dad be dead?*

'Carolyn, I'm sorry...' Simon, her husband, now took the

receiver.

'What happened, Simon? How did he die?'

'We're not exactly sure at this point. The hospital just rang – they said his blood sugars suddenly went very erratic because of the diabetes and they couldn't stabilise him. They couldn't clear his lung because he was paralysed and … well, I'm really sorry, Carolyn. I don't have any more information at this point. I'll call when I know more.'

I put the phone down slowly, carefully. I couldn't believe it. For a moment, I just sat there, breathing hard, trying to take in what I'd just been told. Then, I crumpled over in agony as if I'd been punched in the stomach. My whole body went into shock and I lay on the bed, great big sobs consuming me, pain like I'd never known in my life before. Raymond was also shocked and upset. He had been close to my dad. When I told him I needed to go home right away he said he would get his PA to sort it all out.

'But I can't come,' he said. 'You know I've been organising this banking conference for months now and I can't just drop everything at the last minute.'

'What? Not even for the funeral?' I said, incredulous. 'Just a couple of days. You don't need to be there the rest of the time….'

'It's just not possible.'

'It's my dad, Raymond!'

'I did everything for your dad while he was alive,' Raymond said resolutely. 'He doesn't need me at his funeral.'

I didn't have the strength to argue. Raymond made the arrangements for me and the kids, organising a chauffeur to pick us up at Heathrow and take us back to Peterborough.

'I'm not in a good way,' I felt obliged to tell the smartly-dressed driver when he met us at the arrivals lounge. 'My dad's died and I've come back home.'

'It's okay…' he said kindly as he loaded our bags into the car.

THE WATER RABBIT

'Just take it easy.'

I was usually a nervous passenger, preferring to drive myself, but now I slumped gratefully into the back of the car as we shot up the motorway and I thought back to our trip to Scotland two summers ago. As had become the norm, it was just me and the kids on the long summer holiday back in the UK. Though we had taken a few trips as a family with Raymond, last-minute issues always came up at work and even when he was with us, he was usually preoccupied or on the phone. This time I'd planned a special trip to Scotland with Dad and the kids, now 12, 10 and 8 years old. We'd taken a train up to Edinburgh then hired a car and driven round Scotland. We saw the Edinburgh Tattoo which Dad loved, visited Loch Ness, went to a tartan specialist and took a trip around a distillery where Dad told the kids all about whiskey as he'd been in the wines and spirits trade.

We even visited the site of the crash on the A9 where I'd nearly lost my life aged seven. It had been our last trip together as a family before my parents' marriage fell apart and we had been staying at a campsite in the Outer Hebrides. There, we became friendly with another family at the campsite, a German couple with two kids, a girl and a boy. Their daughter was between mine and my sister's age. We all got on quite well so I started riding in their car to give a bit more space on the backseat of our car for Andrew, Elizabeth and Andrew's friend Neil, who had joined us for the holiday. We had stayed on the Isle of Skye and then taken the ferry back to the mainland together. Now we were touring Scotland as two families and the German family were due to follow us back to Cheshire and stay with us there.

One day, we were coming down the A9 near Pitlochry with my dad driving ahead of us along the twisty, mountain road and I was squashed up on the backseat of the German family's car – a Citroen Dyane 6, a very flimsy car, like deckchairs with a roof.

The journey took a long time and I was so busy staring at the back of Dad's car that I memorised the registration plate as we were driving: MBW 635L. At some point, somewhere along the mountain, we got separated. A few vehicles came between us and I lost sight of Dad's car. Then, as we rounded a bend at speed we veered over the white line into the oncoming lane and at that moment I saw an articulated lorry heading straight towards us. The last thing that went through my mind before impact was — *we're going to hit this lorry.* I closed my eyes and I heard the screeching of brakes and that's all I remember until I came to.

The car ploughed into the lorry. I was knocked unconscious and when I woke up all I could see around me was the car roof. I tried to move but my face was in agony. Somehow, I fell out of the car and as I did, the car door fell off with me. Everything seemed to happen in slow motion. I saw the German father standing up against the wall, he'd lacerated his arm, and somebody was trying to stem the flow of blood. I looked back — the whole car had disintegrated around us. There was nothing left that was bigger than a mobile phone, it was just in bits everywhere. The little girl who had been sitting in the front, had gone through the windscreen and was thrown up the street. The little boy was next to me and he got away with just a graze because he was sheltered under where I had been sitting. The mother had also been thrown up the road, breaking nearly every bone in her body. Meanwhile, the lorry driver was climbing out of his cab with some damage to his chest. The impact had sent the lorry careering towards the edge of the cliff and now the vehicle was hanging half off the mountainside, though thankfully the front part with the cab was still on the road.

I was in shock. I didn't realise it at the time but my face had been bashed in by the contact with the seat in front, with my lower teeth breaking through the skin below my mouth. Two

THE WATER RABBIT

women now came and dragged me away from the wreckage, laying me across the backseat of their car while they waited for the ambulance. *My dad will be worried about me*, I thought.

'Please,' I tried to say to the women. 'You have to get my Dad, you have to get my Dad. MBW 635L. MBW 635L...' I kept repeating the number plate.

As it happened my dad had driven a mile down the road and realised that the traffic waiting to go up was building and there were no cars coming down behind him. So he pulled over to the side of the road and waited. Gradually, it became obvious that something had happened. My dad was not an athletic person but he got out the car and ran all the way back up the hill. At the time I had a colourful, flowery anorak and it was still hanging out of the debris of the Citroen. Now I watched as my dad ran up and stopped near the wreckage of the car, next to my anorak. He went completely white. Even though he was huffing and puffing from running up the hill, the blood drained from his face and he started to shake.

'That's my dad! That's my dad!' I shouted to the lady in the car.

She wound down the window, waved him over and when he saw me, he burst out crying.

'Dad, I'm okay,' I told him as he leant over the car, sobbing.

'I thought we'd lost you,' he wept with relief. 'I thought we'd lost you.'

It was hardly surprising. When you looked at the state of the car, you would never have imagined anybody could have walked away from it. Thankfully, all the members of the German family survived, although the mother was in hospital, covered head to toe plaster in Scotland for six months. I was taken to hospital to be assessed and thankfully, though my face was bruised and swollen, there was no need of surgery. We were housed at the Pitlochry Hotel by the owners, a lovely couple who had kids of their own and took pity on us. Over the next few days we were back and forth to the hospital to visit the little girl and her mother. Meanwhile, news of the horrific car crash was covered in the national press. My mother bought a doll for the German girl, and when I asked her if I could I have one too, she said: 'Well, I suppose so.... but you're not sick, are you?'

I had just survived a terrible car accident, my face was swollen and discoloured on one side and my teeth were knocked through my chin, yet to my mother's mind, I was not deserving of a doll...

Finally, it came time to leave Scotland and drive back to Cheshire.

'I don't want to go in the car, don't make me go in the car,' I said to Dad, terrified.

'Carolyn, it will be okay,' he tried to reassure me.

'No. It won't be okay. It won't. Please, Dad, put me on the train.'

'I promise you,' he broke down crying. 'I promise you, Carolyn. I'll keep you safe.'

I have never been more scared in my entire life than when I had to get back in the car for that long journey to Cheshire. But true to his word, Dad drove us slowly and safely back home.

The trauma of the accident greatly impacted me throughout my life, but it also said so much about my childhood. For one thing, it was always my dad that took care of me. Always. He looked after all three of us and we knew we could put our trust in him. He would never abandon us, no matter what happened. Returning to the site of the crash with him the previous summer had felt calming. So much had happened since that fateful day. I was surprised to see that the stone wall which the car rammed into all those years before had never been repaired. There were still large stones missing. Dad stood, staring at it and quietly said: 'I thought we'd lost you that day, Carolyn.'

The bond between me and Dad had always been good but the crash had been a defining moment. He was my anchor – strong, solid and reliable. It was hard now to believe he was gone and it was I who had lost him.

Once we reached Peterborough, we were caught up in a whirl of activity as arrangements were made for the funeral. My sister and I talked late into the night — she blamed herself for telling me not to come home but I didn't, not for a second. We make our own decisions in life and at least I was spared seeing my dad paralysed after the stroke. I only had good memories of him. For the funeral we asked congregants not to buy flowers – the three of us agreed they were waste of money – but we did dress the coffin with yellow roses, as yellow was the sign of friendship. When the pallbearers took the coffin out of the hearse, a little yellow rosebud rolled off the coffin and dropped on the floor, next to where we were standing. The pallbearer immediately picked it up and gave it to Hannah.

'Grandad wants you to have that,' he said.

'Thank you, I'm putting it in my journal,' she replied. It was a lovely, precious moment in an otherwise bleak day. We three siblings cried the whole way through the service. Dad's old friends had made long journeys to be there. Simon read a heartfelt eulogy that spoke of his love and loyalty to his family and I felt that overall, we did Dad proud. Mum had sent each of us a card, acknowledging that although her marriage to dad had ended long ago, she was sorry for our loss. She wanted to come to the funeral but we wouldn't allow it after the way she treated Dad over the years. Past experience taught us that we couldn't trust her to behave with decorum.

I had been true to my resolution on leaving the UK and not once contacted my mother after that final row. It had caused problems for my siblings, of course, my mother complaining endlessly to my sister about my 'cruel' behaviour but I couldn't let her back into my life just to make things easier for Elizabeth. Honestly, I was much happier without having to deal with my mother. I thought back now to all those years we had been on our own with Dad. It was very unusual back then to be brought up by a single father without the mother dying – we were an anomaly in our community. But he always did his best, fumbling through parenthood with very little direction or help. His own mother had died of breast cancer when he was eight years old. He had been brought up by his father who was a very stern man. I never met him because he died before my mum and dad got married. So my dad had very little experience of a happy family life. He absolutely adored my mum, he was besotted with her, so he did everything possible to try to keep her happy. It was the tragedy of his life that the marriage failed and he showed no interest in relationships after that.

As we were growing up my father set high expectations of us but he struggled to communicate with teenage girls, often coming across as critical. He wasn't keen on my first boyfriend and that really upset me at the time. I didn't like the idea that he questioned my judgement about someone whom I really liked.

'Right, I'll finish with him then,' I told my dad.

'No, don't do that. I'm sorry, Carolyn. You have to make your own choices. Besides, it's not like I'm a shining example of success with relationships.'

He was humble and honest and he always tried his best. The fact was, we meant everything to him but he had no experience, no parenting model, and no one to help or guide him apart from my mother's parents, who became his surrogate parents after

THE WATER RABBIT

Mum left. They lived around forty-five minutes away and came over every Wednesdays and Sundays. Wednesdays quickly became my favourite day of the week, the only day we came home from school to a cooked dinner and fresh-baked cakes, rather than having to prepare food for ourselves.

It was after the funeral and I was still in Peterborough, sorting through Dad's things, when Raymond called me up to ask: 'What do you think of us buying a yacht?'

The question didn't come completely out of the blue. By then we had taken a few sailing holidays together and we were both interested in learning to sail. But buying our own yacht was a massive commitment, both financially and in terms of responsibility. We had kicked the idea around a few times before but neither of us came to a decision. Now I knew my answer.

'Well look, if you want a yacht, buy a yacht,' I replied. If nothing else my dad's shocking demise demonstrated that life was for living. There was no point waiting around for the things we wanted to do. And I could see there might be advantages. Sailing could bring us closer together as a family, Raymond and I might spend more time together. So he placed the order for our yacht and I came back to Hong Kong.

Life quickly returned to normal in Hong Kong. It was probably easier for me than my siblings because Dad and I lived so far apart but he was never far from my thoughts. One night, Dad appeared to me in a very vivid dream. It was a lovely dream – one where we were just sat side by side on a bench together, chatting about all sorts of things, and I felt very happy to be there in his company.

After a while he said: 'Well, you need to go back now, Carolyn.'

'But, Dad, we're not finished talking…'

'Yes, but I'll see you again,' he said.

I wanted to stay, I wanted to stay by his side and keep talking as long as I could but then I woke up.

9

THE RESCUE BEGINS

31 December 2007, South China Sea

IT WAS AFTER midday by the time the tanker was close enough for us to see the crew moving around on board. If this ship seemed big from a distance, up close it was enormous, completely dwarfing our little yacht. The deck of the ship rose at least forty feet into the air, like a block of flats, and when we were alongside we could barely see what was happening on deck, only the preparations with the rescue craft which was winched over the side. We had a plan. Captain Sirpreet had communicated it to me in their approach to our yacht. By now our satellite phone had also stopped working so we were communicating on our VHF radio. He would bring the *Maersk Princess* as close to the yacht as possible, lower their gangway and rope ladder then launch their rescue boat. We would each get into the rescue boat which would then be brought alongside the tanker where we could climb onboard via the rope ladder and gangplank. It made good sense. These large ships were accustomed to bringing local pilots onboard this way when they entered certain ports and had to navigate tricky entranceways. But I was in no doubt this was going to prove very precarious in the open sea with waves building upwards of four metres.

Around a dozen of the crew were now on deck preparing for

the launch of the craft, with three wearing orange foul weather gear and orange life vests on top of that. I guessed these were the men who would be operating the rescue boat. Every single one of the crew on deck also wore a pale blue hard hat. This was by no means a standard operation and there were serious risks involved.

'*Purple X*, we have a problem,' Captain Sirpreet's voice now came on the line. 'The sea is too rough to lower the gangplank. If we put it down now it's just going to smash against the hull and damage the ship. We can only put down the rope ladder. That means your crew will have to get from the rescue boat onto the ladder and climb all the way up to the deck.'

'Understood, Captain.'

'Right now we are preparing the rescue boat. Please standby and prepare to send your first three members of the crew. They will need to jump in the water and swim to the boat.'

'Roger that.' I replied. At this point I was just taking orders and following instructions, which kept me calm.

Sirpreet had previously taken all the details of our crew and ordered Raymond, Martin and Paul to be the first to get in the rescue craft. They would have to climb the rope ladder to the deck. As I understood it, the remainder of our group and the ones considered the weaker members – that is, myself, the boys and Victor – would be hoisted up in the craft.

Eventually, after all the preparations were made, we saw the small orange rescue boat lowered down the side of the hull into the water with three crew members onboard. Once in the sea, the boat was immediately swamped by the large swell. It struggled to motor towards us, getting as close as it could get without risking a collision. Then, when it was around ten metres away, the *Maersk* crew shouted for the three men to jump in and swim towards the rescue boat. Martin went first. I watched as he dived in, his life jacket inflating on impact with the water, and he started to power through the waves. The ocean was a swirling, seething force that pulled and dragged on our small yacht – I wondered how Martin would cope once he was in the water. But he seemed to make good progress and quickly made it across the murky green waves to the boat. He was hauled onboard just as the small life raft was swamped by another big wave. One of the crew was trying to bail out with a bucket at his feet. Martin immediately started bailing, too. Next, they rounded Paul and then Raymond jumped into the water and swam across to the rescue boat. I stood on the deck, watching this all unfold through gritted teeth. It felt as if seeing it all in slow motion. *Come on, Come on, Come on....*

Nothing seemed to happen fast enough. I was willing everyone to get in that rescue boat as fast as possible, desperate for this ordeal to be over.

Once all three were aboard, the rescue craft got as close to the tanker as it dared without hitting it. I thought at this point the men would be brought alongside the tanker to reach the ladder by standing in the rescue boat. But the waves were too large and there was no way the rescue boat could get close to the tanker. It looked like there was some discussion onboard and then we saw Martin jumping off the rescue boat and into the water, heading straight for the rope ladder on the tanker. I held my breath. All he had to do was get a hand on the bottom rung of the ladder then he would be able to pull himself up to climb. But it looked impossible, even from where I was standing. The rope ladder was not designed to be reached from the water but from a boat. It simply didn't stretch far enough, even when the tanker lurched towards him in the waves. If anyone could do it, it would be Martin – physically, he was probably the fittest of us all. Now, as the tanker rolled towards him and the mauve hull disappeared below the water line, Martin took his chance. He reached an arm up towards the ladder and his fingertips just touched the bottom rung but he didn't manage to get his whole hand on it and he fell instantly backwards into the water. Now the current carried him back towards the stern of the ship.

'Martin!' I screamed out in terror. He was heading straight for the propeller! If they didn't cut the engines immediately he would be dragged through. *No. No. No. This can't happen. This just can't happen.* It all happened so quickly – if they didn't act within a second Martin would be killed. I heard urgent shouts from the deck of the tanker – they could see where he was headed and the message was relayed to the Captain to shut the engine down.

Moments later, the engines were shut down. Amongst the noise, I heard Martin shouting his daughter's name, "Ysobelle, Ysobelle!" as the sea bounced him along the hull of the ship and then push off the rudder.

Thank God! Martin floated safely to the rear of the ship just as the engine was cut. I couldn't believe how quickly it had all gone wrong. The carefully planned rescue which Sirpreet had laid out was proving impossible to execute in these conditions. The rescue boat went around to pick Martin up and I wondered what they would try next. Captain Sirpreet came on the radio and said they were going to raise the rescue boat with the passengers still inside using the small cranes onboard the ship.

During this time I still had use of the yacht engine, so I was trying to hold the yacht steady. We were still taking on water but not, it seemed, at a rate that was perilous yet. Ironically, I was starting to feel the rescue itself was becoming very perilous, but if we didn't take the chance of rescue now, where would we be by nightfall? We watched as the rescue boat moved from midships – where the rope ladder was situated – up to the stern and attached at either end to the two steel cables on the cranes so that it could be winched aboard. Once the boat was secured to the wires the cranes wound the steel cables in and the boat slowly began a jerky movement upwards. But the weather conditions made this difficult and we could see the boat swaying in the wind, smacking against the side of the tanker.

About halfway up, the rescue boat suddenly tipped backwards, the front end lifting high up into the air.

'Oh my god!' I exclaimed as I saw the passengers inside slide backwards and fall to the floor of the boat. With six people aboard, it was lucky that none of them fell out! We were alarmed. I held the boys close, trying to steady all our nerves, but this was frightening. Their father was in that boat and right at this minute we had no idea what was happening to him since the craft was too far away and high up for us to see. Later, we discovered it was the weight of the water inside the rescue boat that had made it unstable and, when it was lifted upwards, it wasn't level so the water surged towards the back of the boat, making it tip. In the chaos, Raymond was knocked unconscious, cracking his head on the middle of the boat, breaking his collar bone and gashing his leg open. Martin had to drag him out of the water and give him CPR in the life raft to resuscitate him. Paul was injured too, cracking the base of his back, and one of the Maersk crew members split his head.

Shit shit shit...

This plan wasn't working either. *How are they going to get us all on board?* I wondered. The rescue craft only just reached the deck of the ship, literally hanging by a thread. It was a miracle they made it at all. It seemed that one of the clips to the raft was not properly attached and if that had gone completely, the whole thing would be left hanging by one clip. The boat would have tipped vertically and everybody would have fallen out.

As soon as the rescue craft was on board our crew — as well

as the injured rescue boat operators — were taken to the cafeteria on the ship, which had been transformed into a makeshift triage centre. There were now three seriously injured people aboard.

When Captain Sirpreet finally appeared on the deck with the VHF radio in his hand, it wasn't good news.

'The rescue boat is damaged,' he shouted over the radio. 'We can't use it again so now we're going to send a rocket with a messenger line attached to it. We'll fire the rocket over the deck of the yacht. When we do that you'll have to grab the messenger line and pull it towards you. It will be attached to a life ring which is on a rope attached to the *Maersk*. You will need to send the next crew member in that life ring and we will pull them back to the ship and up onto the rope ladder. They will then climb the rope ladder to the deck. Do you understand?'

'YES!' I shouted back. 'Understood. Standing by for the messenger line.' I was on auto pilot waiting for the next direction.

Next, we heard a shot – like a gunshot – and a small missile flew towards our boat, leaving a trail of white smoke in its wake, just like the flares. The rocket landed on the deck and behind it floated down a pale green line which looked a bit like Silly String. It was lightweight and thin but obviously made of strong stuff. We all grabbed it and started to pull it towards the yacht, eventually seeing the life ring come down from the ship towards us. The hard ring was attached to a polypropylene rope which would be used to drag the crew member back to the ship. There were now four of us on the yacht — me, Victor, Aaron and Joe. I turned to my two sons: 'Okay, it's one of you. Who wants to go first?'

Joe, my youngest, grabbed the ring: 'I'll go first.'

10

Lost

April 2003, Hong Kong

'I'll help you, Mum!' Joe volunteered. 'That looks really fun.'

It was early 2003 and we were planning a holiday for the summer – it looked to be our last big family holiday together, since Hannah would enter the sixth form next year and we expected her to go on the end-of-school trip to Koh Samui. The children had six weeks holiday but we really had to plan around Raymond's work commitments. So after consulting on his dates, it was decided we would visit New Zealand for two weeks. We had previously been on a sailing holiday there and loved it and wanted to go back. The kids were keen on snowboarding and both Raymond and I had longed to see even more of New Zealand. There was a long list of requests of all the things everyone wanted to do, so Joe offered to help make the arrangements.

Together, we trawled the internet and found an online, tailormade holiday planner.

'So you see, Mum, you just put in your budget and then she plans it all for you,' Joe pointed to the website.

'Okay, let's try it. What is our expenditure level – backpack, budget, comfortable or luxury?'

'We might as well go for the top one. Pick luxury!'

THE WATER RABBIT

I clicked on the luxury option and together Joe and I filled in the rest of the online form – yes, we wanted to try adventure sports, yes, we were interested in whale watching and hot air ballooning and glacier hiking. It was so exciting. When the holiday planner eventually came back with our itinerary, it looked amazing. She had organised all these incredible experiences, staying in the best hotels all over the country. It really was a once-in-a-lifetime trip!

The night before the holiday I was busy packing and organising the kids' cases when Raymond called. He had been in Beijing for work and was due to fly back to Hong Kong to travel with us to Auckland the next day. From there we would take an internal flight to start our tour from Christchurch.

'I don't think I'm going to make it,' he said.

'What? What do you mean?' I froze, mid-pack.

'I'm not going to make the holiday.'

I stood there, momentarily stunned into silence, surrounded by piles of clothes and mountains of snowboarding kit. There was no way I was doing this on my own.

'Raymond,' I said quietly. 'You *are* going to make the holiday. These dates are the ones you gave me and it has been booked for months.'

'Yeah, well it would have been better if it had been a week later…'

'Raymond, I can't change it now. It's paid for. It's a lot of money. It's all booked. It's BOOKED, for Christ's sake!'

By now I was starting to shake. My anxiety levels, already high from the stress of packing for five people, shot through the roof and I felt my breathing becoming quick and shallow. *How could he do this to me the night before the holiday?*

'Look, Raymond,' I started again, slightly calmer. 'We can't cancel now. I've got all this bloody luggage and me and the kids are catching a flight to Auckland tomorrow night. You are coming!'

'Hmm... let me see what I can do,' he said and hung up.

I knew this would happen. *I just knew it!* The worst thing about this moment was knowing that I could have predicted it. As was so often the case with our lives now, we would plan something, get ready to do it and then Raymond would bail at the last minute. It was horribly stressful but there was nothing I could do about it. I just got used to being on my own. I actually thought of myself as a single parent these days because I was alone so much. I went to the kids' sporting practices on my own, parents' evenings, the kids' birthday parties and even picked out their birthday presents alone. Raymond did sometimes attend rugby training on a Sunday morning if he was around, but it was a big 'if'.

'We're a great partnership!' Raymond told people. I think he meant that while he earned the money I did everything else. But it didn't feel like a partnership to me. Partners share a life: we didn't share anything together, besides the kids, but even then, I was doing the lion's share of caring. This was the price of a partner of a high-powered investment banker in a city like Hong Kong.

'I don't know about a partnership,' I quipped. 'It feels like you're the director of the company and I'm your personal assistant.'

My friends frequently asked if I was fed up with being on my own.

'Of course I don't like it, but it's his job,' I'd tell them. 'What can I do?'

The fact is that I knew how much he was earning and it seemed surly and ungrateful to complain when your husband was bringing home a stratospheric salary. Being alone was simply the price I paid for that lifestyle and I had to suck it up.

By now, it had been drummed into me that nobody earning that kind of money got to spend time with their family. The life of an investment banker was brutal and cutthroat. Raymond didn't like to talk about his work to anyone – including me – because he didn't trust anyone not to misuse that information. So he maintained a veil of secrecy over his work and I got used to the fact that he didn't talk to me about his professional life anymore.

But as much as I tried to accept these compromises, Raymond was away on business so much I went through long stretches of feeling extremely lonely. I couldn't help it. I had my job as a teaching assistant, the kids, very good friends and a reasonable social life but when you're married, you expect a level of companionship and intimacy that was simply missing from my life. I didn't feel close to Raymond anymore but then I wasn't free to explore closeness elsewhere either. My friends kept me sane but I was still a living, breathing human being with her own needs. I was stuck, and though I knew my marriage wasn't great, it never occurred to me to leave. I didn't want to do what my mother had done to me and my siblings. So life with Raymond was tolerable – lonely and frustrating – but not painful enough to push me into any drastic action.

But dropping out of our New Zealand trip the night before we were due to travel? This was too much. If he didn't come this time, what was the point of being married at all? For the next half an hour, I paced the bedroom, wondering what to do if he didn't make it. There was no question of changing the dates. Should I cancel the holiday? The kids would be devastated – it was all we had talked about for months. If we went alone, then I knew I could manage on my own but it was such a burden. The thought of leading us through two weeks in New Zealand was overwhelming. It was one place after another as we weren't due to stay in the same place for more than a night until we got to

Queenstown for the snowboarding.... Urgh. I felt like crawling under my duvet and spending the next two weeks in bed!

The phone sprang to life.

'Okay. There's a flight to Christchurch via Sydney. It looks like, if my connections go as planned, I'll arrive there about half an hour after you and the kids and then we can travel to the hotel together.'

'Okay, okay...' *Thank god for that!* 'Please try to make that flight, Raymond.'

I still had to take all the luggage with the kids and it wasn't guaranteed he would make the flight, but at least I knew now that he was coming with us.

The next 48 hours were horribly stressful. I got myself, the three kids and all our luggage to Auckland and then transferred to the flight to Christchurch. There were no mobile phones allowed on planes so I couldn't tell if Raymond had made the connecting flight from Sydney. I scanned the Arrivals board. If he was on that plane, we only had an hour's wait but if he was on the next one, arriving at midnight, I'd just have to go to our hotel with the kids and come back for him.

I went up to the Qantas desk to beg for information.

'Look, I know you're not meant to tell me who is on the flight because of security, but I've got my three kids here and all this baggage and my husband is meant to be coming in from Sydney so could you at least tell me if he made the plane? If he hasn't, I'll take the kids to the hotel.'

'I'm sorry, we're not allowed to give out that information.'

I tried Raymond's mobile again. He didn't answer – did that mean he was on the plane? I must have looked fairly upset because the guy on the Qantas desk took pity on me and said: 'I'd look towards the Cinderella hour if I was you.'

That means midnight.... so he didn't make the plane!

THE WATER RABBIT

Thankfully, he made it by midnight and said he'd take a taxi to our hotel so I wouldn't have to go back to collect him. It wasn't a good way to start any holiday.

But what was most hurtful was that he seemed resigned about not going away with us, his family. I had had to read him the riot act to get him along and that was exhausting. Why couldn't he just tell his company that he was going on holiday and let them deal with things while he was away? To my mind, if someone was at the very top of their profession, then they held a certain amount of power and had the ability to set the parameters of their working life. I didn't understand why he couldn't or wouldn't do that. He just never really seemed overly concerned about missing out on our time together. The upshot was my constant sense of being unimportant in his life, an inconvenience.

I was usually a very organised person and liked things to go according to plan. But now Raymond's job took precedence on every occasion and I was constantly on edge that things were going to change at the last minute. If I ever brought this up or talking about being on my own, he would accuse me of giving him 'extra stress.... and aren't I stressed enough already?'

So I stopped 'complaining' and slowly, over time, our conversations changed. The kids would soon be going off to university, living independent lives, and then I would be on my own completely. I felt that our marriage had suffered enough as a result of his work.

'Raymond, why don't you think about quitting your job?' I suggested. 'We don't need any more money. We've got more than enough money to send the kids through university and it would be nice to be together as a family before they leave home.'

We lived on a beautiful houseboat that Raymond had helped design, we owned some property. Judging from the last few years' salary, I knew we must be doing well. To my mind,

Raymond could easily change jobs or retire and we would still be very comfortable for the rest of our lives. But he wasn't prepared to consider quitting.

'Why would I do that?' he said. 'I can't do this job forever. I'm going to do it as long as I can do it. It won't be for much longer.'

'How much longer though? I don't want to have this conversation again in five years.'

'I don't know what you're talking about...'

'I'm fed up, Raymond! I'm lonely and I'm bloody fed up. There's more to life than money. Yes, we had financial concerns back in the day, but not anymore. We can live with less stress about work and money if we choose to.'

But Raymond just shrugged it all off. To him, I was just being awkward and annoying.

Over the next couple of years, my mood sank lower and lower. It felt like I was the problem. The kids and Raymond seemed happy enough and my misery was getting everyone down. If I didn't feel in the mood to do things, I was accused of spoiling the fun for the others. And what was wrong with me anyway? In 2005, Hannah left home to start at Durham University. She was ready to go but her absence left a gap in my life. I missed her desperately, I missed her feistiness. The boys were doing their own thing, Raymond was around less and less and when he was home, he was so busy he didn't have time for me. It felt like we were all on a fairground carousel; everybody going round and round on the horses, enjoying the ride, except me. I was the only one who wanted to get off, but in order to get off, we'd have to stop the ride and spoil everyone's fun. I was functional, I still held down a job and ran the household but inside, it felt like I was dying.

Over the years I retreated into myself but when it all got too much I went to the doctors. I had lost interest in all things that used to give me pleasure. I didn't want to go out to meet friends anymore. I was tired all the time. I stopped eating proper meals, just a biscuit in the morning and a tiny bowl of rice with vegetables for dinner. I had no appetite and felt a constant pressure inside, that at any moment I would crumple. I had no joy. Everything was a huge effort and seemed grey in meaning and as well as colour. At times, I felt I was on the verge of tears. I felt confused and couldn't reconcile the way my life looked to others and the reality of the misery I felt. The doctor diagnosed me with clinical depression and prescribed antidepressants.

One day, in August 2005, I was swimming in the pool of the Marina Club and I felt overcome by misery. I dunked my head under the water and held my breath. *I don't want to be here anymore. I just want to disappear.* My daughter was on a university field trip to Iceland, Joe was on holiday with a friend in the south of France, Aaron was at summer school at Stanford University in the US and Raymond was in Shanghai on business. I could go anywhere in the world... anywhere! And I could go first class if I wanted because, well, we had the money. But today, like all the other days, it was a struggle just to get out of bed. *What was the point? What was the point in any of it?* I was lonely, adrift in my life, and I didn't know what to do with myself anymore.

Under the water, I held my breath as I scissored my legs through the water, then I came up for air. *Is this what life is all about? Do I keep just taking the pills forever?* I swam to the edge of the pool and grabbed onto the side. Then I pushed off again and let myself glide under the water. Again, I came up for breath. *No, I can't go on like this. I have money, I can find somebody to help me.* When I first went to the doctor he said the pills would help me. I believed it was just a blip and maybe my age or 'empty nest' syndrome. But I didn't want to take pills forever. Maybe it was time to find someone to talk to.

I had never imagined having therapy before now. To my mind it was something for people with real problems or for the extremely self-indulgent. Where I came from, you didn't complain or voice your emotions, you just get on with it. It felt like a very drastic step, employing someone to listen to my problems, but by now I really had nothing to lose. I didn't want to be on pills for the rest of my life. Overcoming my prejudices and preconceptions about therapy was the first step on my road to recovery. So I looked around and found a therapist who I started to see in January 2006, twice a week at first. We talked a lot about my upbringing – something I had never really done before. For years, I had buried the trauma of my past in my shiny new life but he helped me to understand how my past had led me to this point.

I had never been encouraged to express my feelings as a child. When I lay on the sofa, crying with agony, I had been told to just 'shut up'. And that's how I got used to living my life. Besides, my mum had more emotional outbursts than the whole family put together. She did the emotion for us all. After growing up with her drama and all the chaos she left in her wake, I just wanted peace and calm. I looked to my Grandma for a role model. My mother's mother was a short Yorkshire lady, a solid, low-key character who put up with my mother's erratic and selfish behaviour with strength and stoicism.

Talking about what I had been through as a child and how it affected me as an adult was critical and now I could look at my fears and demons to figure out who I was and why I felt like I did. When I talked to my therapist about Raymond, he suggested we attend marriage counselling together, but Raymond rejected that idea.

'I haven't got time,' he objected. That was hurtful. If he wasn't willing to work on our marriage, there was very little I could do about it. Instead, I focused on myself.

By August 2006 I was starting to feel much better.

'I think you've come a long way,' said my therapist and he was right. By now I was only seeing him once a week. I felt stronger, better able to cope, so I came off the antidepressants and signed up for night classes for a degree in Criminology.

'Why are you wasting your time with that?' Raymond said when I told him about my plans to go to university. He'd never asked about my therapy, he didn't seem interested.

'Well, I've always been fascinated by crime...'

'What's the point? You don't need a degree now...'

'Well, maybe I don't *need* a degree, but I want to get one. I can afford to do it. I've got the time and we've got the money. This is something I want to do for me, Raymond. I never did go to university and at the time I felt that it wasn't the right time for me. But now feels like a good time.'

'Well, you better make it worthwhile then,' he sniffed. 'You better get a first class honours.'

My marriage was tolerable. It wasn't what I had imagined twenty years earlier but then nobody claimed a long marriage was all romance and roses. We'd built a great life together and I had made peace with the compromises we had made to get here. I knew that once the kids were gone, we could figure out how we were going to bring ourselves back together. We could move into a different phase and recreate what we had lost along the way. Life could definitely be worse. I had friends, I occupied my mind with edifying activities and enjoyed a fulfilling job. I was resilient and resourceful. Most of all, I felt hopeful once again.

11

IN THE SEA

31 December 2007, South China Sea

Nothing on earth could have prepared me for watching my youngest child jump into the gigantic, raging ocean. It was a truly terrible moment. Joe had volunteered to be the first to go across on the life belt attached to the ship and even offered to take our Grab Bag with him. This was the bright yellow waterproof bag containing all our passports and emergency documents. We had asked Captain Sirpreet if we were allowed to bring some possessions on board and he said we could take a small bag each so we had lashed a few bags together onto a rope and at the end I attached the empty flare box containing Aaron's expensive camera and all our cash.

'I love you,' I whispered as I held my youngest son close. 'You can do it, Joe.'

'I love you too, Mum.'

He lifted the life belt over his head and turned to me deadly serious: 'You must save yourselves. Forget the bags, just save yourselves.'

Then he jumped.

My heart pounded as I watched my sixteen-year-old disappear below the waves. His self-inflating life jacket puffed up around his neck as it made contact with the water, bringing him back to

THE WATER RABBIT

the surface again. The crew aboard the *Maersk Princess* wound the rope back towards them and Joe made quick progress to the rope ladder at the bottom of the tanker. Silhouetted against the giant tanker, my son looked so small. It was a long way from the bottom of the ladder up to the deck and the first thing he needed to do was get on it. I was transfixed, not daring to blink, as I willed my son to get his hand on the ladder. He was a fit lad, he played a lot of rugby, and I knew that if he could just get a hand on the ladder he would be capable of climbing to the top. But first he had to get on. *Come on Joe, Come on Joe. You can do it.* The crew appeared to wait until the tanker heeled towards him then, just at the moment it tipped, the life belt jerked upwards and Joe reached up, grabbing hold of the bottom rung. *Yes! He's got it.* Now he scrambled to get both hands and feet on the ladder and all of us — onboard the yacht and tanker –started to shout: 'Come on! Come on!' Joe shot up that ladder like a monkey – and the crew kept pace with him, winding the rope at the same time so that it was always taut. When he clambered onboard, I felt myself finally letting out a breath. *Thank God, he's safe!*

The rescue crew sent a second rocket with another messenger line. The rocket shot over the deck, landing in the sea, just as before, and the messenger fluttered down onto the deck. Aaron would go next. We got hold of the thin line and started to pull, dragging the life ring and rope towards us. When Aaron put the life ring over his head I said to him: 'Now please be careful.'

'For god's sake, Mum!' he snapped back, irritated by my fussing.

Why did I tell him to be careful? I hadn't said it to Joe. I guess my stress levels were rising all the time. Would our luck run out? I just kept waiting for things to get worse.

'You can do it. Joe did it.'

'Yeah, I can do it. I know I can do it,' he swatted me away, like an annoying fly, then he jumped in the water. Once again I watched as my son was dragged across the ocean to the rope ladder. I was just terrified that fate would catch up with us and stop us in our tracks. It felt like holding on for dear life to something with my arms aching, knowing that I have to let go imminently. He made a grab for the bottom rung as the ship heeled towards him. It was low enough for him to scramble onto the first rung. *Yes, he's got it!*

He pulled himself up and once his feet were on the ladder he started to climb, just as his brother had done. *Come on, Aaron! Come on!* My eyes were on him the whole time. I couldn't look away until I knew he was safe. But when he got about halfway up the ladder, he stopped.

Why is he stopping? Is he okay?

The crew on the *Maersk* also saw he had stopped climbing and they stopped winding the rope. There was an eerie moment of calm. My heart was thudding so hard in my chest I thought it would pop right out. *For God's sake, what wrong? What's wrong?* All I wanted at that moment was to jump in the sea and go and get him. But I knew that would have been a suicidal act of madness. Instead, I bit down hard on my bottom lip and waited. Somebody from the tanker shouted down to see if he was okay and he looked up at them and nodded. *Is he having a rest?* The ladder was really long – the equivalent to four storeys high – and it must have been exhausting to climb up....

'Come on, Aaron. You can do it. You can do it!' I shouted.

The tension was unbearable. How long was he there for? I couldn't tell. Time seemed elastic, stretching out into infinite space. I felt as if we were all suspended in this moment, watching him just hang there like that, knowing that if he dropped into the sea, he could be dragged to the back of the ship. *Would they be able to keep him on the life ring? Was the propeller still going? Would they be able to turn it off if they saw him fall?* All these thoughts raced through my head as I stood there watching him, completely helpless. Eventually, he started climbing again and I felt like crying. He was doing well, going at a fair pace, and it wasn't long before he reached the deck and I watched as the crew members helped him climb aboard the *Maersk*. I wanted to sit down right there and weep with relief. My kids were safe. If nothing else went right today, I knew that at least my children were out of harm's way.

Later, when we spoke about it, Aaron told me he had stopped because the life jacket was pushing him away from the rope ladder, making it hard to climb. At the moment he had hung there, halfway to safety, he had seriously considered getting his pocketknife out of his trousers and stabbing his life jacket to deflate it.

'I nearly did it, Mum,' he said. 'But then I thought better of it. It was difficult on the ladder with my life jacket up around my ears, but I knew that if I punctured the life jacket and fell into the water I would be finished.'

It was now early afternoon and with the majority of our crew onboard the *Maersk*, there was a lull in the weather. Until this point it had been fairly windy and the waves around us were peaking at three metre swells. It hadn't been easy to keep the yacht steady during this time – we still had engine power and I had been steering it, moving it back and forward to ensure we maintained our distance from the tanker. Now, with just me and Victor left onboard *Purple X*, the storm seemed to quiet down.

'Let's send the bags next,' Victor suggested.

'Forget the bags,' I said. 'We just need to get off this boat.'

'I want my bag.'

It was a tricky moment. I didn't want to be the one to tell Victor he couldn't have his bag. We had brought him on this trip. It was entirely due to us that he was now in this perilous situation, but at the same time I felt strongly that Joe was right, we were still in immense danger and had to focus on saving ourselves. The Captain appeared on deck. I chose to leave the decision up to him; after all, he was in charge of this rescue.

'Can we send the bags next, Captain?' I shouted from the yacht to ship.

By now the battery had died on our VHF radio because we couldn't charge it so our only way to communicate was to shout at each other.

'Your lives are more important,' he yelled back.

'But it's not that windy now.'

He threw his hands in the air, as if to say: 'What the hell!'

So they sent another rocket across, we caught the messenger line and pulled in their rope, this time with no life ring. We attached our rope with the string of bags to theirs and Victor and I tossed all the bags in the sea. They started to winch the rope in and the line of bags bobbed along the water and then dragged up the side of the ship. It was a surreal scene, watching this line of bags being hauled up the side of the ship like a string of Christmas baubles. *Why am I watching these bags being rescued?* I wondered to myself. It seemed to take forever and at one stage it appeared as if the crew stopped winching. Perhaps the bags were now much heavier from getting wet. As the bags hung there, I noticed a light flashing from inside one of them. It was one of the strobe lights we wore round our necks at night. It had activated on contact with the water, flashing inside the bag. *Now, what's the bloody point in that?* It was one of those stupid moments in life that make you wonder if you're going mad. Right in the middle of an absolute crisis I was watching a string of bags being rescued. It was ridiculous!

Finally, the bags jerked their way up to the deck of the tanker.

But on one of the big tugs, the flare box at the bottom dropped off the end of the rope and was swept away. *Damn it!* The one thing that felt like it was worth saving – the box contained all our cash and the good camera with the photos — was gone. With the wind now building again, I had just one thought; with only me and Victor left onboard, who would go first? It should probably be Victor. As the owner of *Purple X*, I assumed that I had to remain on board until the last member of crew was rescued in order to keep the yacht steady. When they finished pulling the bags on deck the Captain shouted down to us: 'We're going to send two lines now. You will both come together at the same time.'

Thank god! That was a huge relief. I would have volunteered to be the last person on *Purple X*, but I was still scared to be alone.

By now the wind had picked up again and it was blowing a gale. Another two rockets were fired and the messenger lines landed on our deck – one after the other. We made a grab for the thin lines that fluttered down behind the rockets. It was very impressive that every single rocket had been fired with such precision that each line landed perfectly on our yacht. I imagine it wasn't an easy task, considering the wind, the waves, the distance between our vessels and the fact that we were two moving objects in the water.

We pulled the rings towards us and just before I put mine over my head, I said to Victor: 'I'm going to switch off the engine and turn the wheel so the yacht steers away from the tanker. I'll lock the wheel in that position.'

It was over. Our adventures with *Purple X* had well and truly come to an end and abandoning ship meant almost certainly we would never see her again. My heart was heavy at that thought. *Purple X* was a beautiful boat. We had been on many adventures with her and she had been our home, our haven, during this trip. As much as I wanted to get off this yacht and onto the safety of the tanker, I was sad to see her go. I switched off the engine for the last time, locked the steering wheel in place and put the ring over my head.

'Okay?' Victor asked.

I nodded and we jumped in the sea.

I felt the shock of cold water rushing over my body and gasped. Suddenly my life vest inflated, popping open around my neck. Everything now felt very real. I was no longer standing on a dry yacht, watching the water below my feet, I was in the cold ocean, with the giant tanker rising up in front of me and a life vest around my neck restricting all my movement.

They dragged us to the side of the ship. I was staring up at the ladder, and the intimidatingly high climb to get to the top of it. *Oh my god.* I was overwhelmed at the magnitude of the task. From the water, it seemed so very high up. *If the kids can do it, I can do it. Or can I? Can I get on that rope ladder? I just have to get on it... once I'm on I'll start climbing and they'll start pulling.*

But there was only one rope ladder and there were two of us in the water so one of us had to go first. Both Victor and I were being held against the side of the ship by the ropes attached to the life rings. I was closer to the ladder – Victor was slightly behind me — so I went for it first.

I got to the rope ladder and on my first attempt, I managed to touch the bottom rung but my fingers weren't high enough to get a grip and I fell back in the water. Just at that moment, I saw our yacht rounding up and bumping back along the side of the tanker, bashing its way down from the bow towards us. The steering was locked in position so it couldn't move away from the tanker. It just kept bumping against it, getting closer and closer... I was directly in its path but I was held, pinned against the side of the ship. Unless I got out of the way fast, I was going to be sandwiched between the two vessels.

'You've got to let me go,' I shouted up at the crew. 'Please. Let me go. I'm going to be crushed. Let me go!'

This was a nightmare scenario. I was tethered tightly to the side of the ship, just sitting there, waiting to be smashed against the tanker by my own yacht.

'LET ME GO!' I screamed again, desperate now. I had to get away so I could push myself away from the ship. Our yacht weighed 23 tonnes; there was no way I would survive being squashed between that and the ship. So the crew let the line out and I managed to push myself along the side of the tanker to the stern where the rudder was, just as the yacht came towards my face and then over my left shoulder. It was so close it came within inches of hitting me. I thought I was going to be crushed to death. By now, Victor was behind me, way behind me, not anywhere near the ship. They had to let his line out too, so he could scramble out of the way of the yacht. My last vision of *Purple X* was the back end of it coming towards me and then I never saw it again.

The immediate danger was over but during this time the tanker had been moving forwards, just as Victor and I were moving backwards, dragged by the current. The tanker was getting further and further away from us both. Victor and I found each other at the back of the ship where he had also swum for safety from the yacht, but with every second the tanker seemed to move further into the distance. I wasn't panicked though. We still had hold of the nylon rope attaching us to the ship.

I could see people running backwards and forwards over the back of the ship and read the lettering over the stern: *Maersk Princess*. But the tanker didn't stop. It just kept getting further away from us, those words disappearing off into the distance.

'We have to pull ourselves back to the ship,' I said to Victor.

'But we're not attached anymore...'

'Just pull the rope!' I said urgently.

So we kept pulling and pulling. There must have been about 200 yards of rope but it was like one of those *Tom and Jerry* cartoons, where Tom runs a rope through his hands and gets to the end only to find it's not attached to anything. Only this wasn't a punchline, it was a disaster.

'Oh my god, Victor!'

'We're not attached to anything...' he said again.

I looked up and the ship was gone. It had completely disappeared from our view. We could now see very little except the water around us since the waves were huge. We were lost at sea.

12

May Day

31 December 2007, South China Seas

'We have to get rid of this rope...' I said to Victor. There was so much blue polypropylene rope floating around us in the water we were becoming dangerously entangled with it.

'Pull the life ring off...' he suggested. The rope was attached to the life rings so the only way to get rid of all the rope was to take off our life rings. It seemed counter-intuitive to ditch the rings but the rope was so all encompassing and tangling us up that we were like fish in a net. Bobbing in the huge swell, we needed all our limbs to tread water. It was not possible to stay afloat and start undoing ropes and rings.

Now we had our life jackets but no life rings and we linked arms to ensure we didn't lose one another and to help keep each other afloat. My mind suddenly flashed back to a documentary I'd seen during my high school days when a sailor had fallen off the back of a US aircraft carrier into the Indian Ocean. He'd managed to save himself by taking off his trousers and tying knots in the bottom of the legs, flicking them over his head and wearing them as a makeshift life preserver. This was just what we'd been taught in our school lifesaving classes. In his case, the aircraft carrier turned around and came back to rescue him and he lived to tell his story.

'It's a terrible feeling watching the ship disappear off into the horizon. And you're just left there.' His words came back to me at this moment. *My god, I know exactly what he means. We are literally stuck here, two tiny specks of humanity in this vast, tempestuous ocean.* I too had never felt so desolate or small. We could see nothing but sea and by this time the waves were very big, ten metre swells from the start of the crest of the wave to the bottom. There was no way we could swim with life jackets and foul weather gear on. In this stormy ocean, we were just bobbing around, moving wherever the water took us. It was as much as we could manage to tread water and keep ourselves on the surface. I tried to stay positive.

'They'll come back for us,' I said to Victor as we struggled against the waves. Each time we got to the bottom of a swell we sank under the water, sea water shot up my nose and straight into my stomach. Then I came up to the surface, vomited up water, breathed out and grabbed some more air, just before we were plunged under the water again. This happened over and over again. The waves were rough, we were getting sucked up and down. Occasionally, I opened my eyes under the water and it was like looking through the door of a washing machine: the water swirling all around me. I was constantly out of breath, spluttering continuously. No sooner had I retched up the water than it was filling up my guts again. *How long can we go on like this? What the hell's happened to the ship?*

I found out later that aboard the *Maersk* they upgraded our distress call to a May Day. Since we were now lost at sea there was an imminent danger to life and unless we got help very soon, we weren't going to survive. The May Day went out to all the ships in the area. We were later told that the captain of another large vessel, a car transporter, *Clipper Lagoon*, was in the area and responded. In a bizarre twist of fate, the *Clipper Lagoon* captain had actually trained Captain Sirpreet and though they had known each other many years earlier they hadn't seen each other in eighteen years.

The *Maersk Princess* turned around and now every member of the crew desperately scanned the ocean, searching for us. Meanwhile, one deck below, in the cafeteria area where they had set up a triage centre, the two boys – Aaron and Joe – were still unaware of the unfolding horror. For a long time, they sat there, expecting me and Victor to join them at any moment. But time passed and we didn't appear. Raymond and Paul were unable to stand due to their serious injuries.

'Where's my mum?' Joe asked one of the crew. 'Why is it taking so long to get my mum onto the ship?'

Nobody responded to their questions so they went up to the bridge. Martin joined them, also concerned for me and Victor, but none of them were allowed on the bridge. Eventually, Martin entered the bridge, demanding to know what was happening.

'We don't know where they are,' the second officer admitted.

'What do you mean you don't know where they are?' He was staggered.

'We've lost them. We can't find them. We had to let out the lines when the yacht came back. If we hadn't let them out they would have been crushed against the ship. But they were swept away by the currents and now we can't find them.'

I cannot imagine how my sons must have felt at that moment, knowing that there was a possibility they may never see me again.

The message was relayed back to the rescue coordination team in Hong Kong that two of the crew of *Purple X* were lost at sea. Hannah was also given the message, though neither person was identified to her. It was both too much and too little information at the same time. Was it her mother lost at sea, her father, her two brothers? Could she be an orphan before the New Year? Or perhaps they were two unrelated members of the crew. She didn't know how to feel. She was totally in the dark. Only one thing was certain – she could do absolutely nothing about it. All she could do was sit and wait for more news. I don't know what she went through during those terrible hours, but I'm certain it must have been highly traumatic.

How on earth are they going to find us? I wondered, bleakly. It was around 3pm, all I could do was try to stay alive and hope they would come back for us, but the current was moving at quite a speed and we kept getting sucked under the water, coming up again a couple of hundred yards away from where we had been before. We were surrounded by miles and miles of ocean and we were just two tiny bodies, being tossed around in the waves. Every minute in that water felt like an hour, every second a desperate struggle for air and survival.

It was a daunting task to try and find us but just over two hours later there was a breakthrough on the *Maersk*. One of the crew was looking out the window with binoculars when he spotted a tiny yellow dot. The flare box! Whatever direction the flare box had drifted in, we would have been dragged in the same direction, too, because you can't fight against the current. So they tracked the flare box and set a course in that direction. Half a mile beyond the yellow box they spotted two little black dots. Our heads! Who would ever have imagined we would be saved by that happy accident of the flare box dropping into the ocean? Every single person on the bridge, including several with binoculars, was instructed not to take their eyes off us.

At this time, the *Clipper Lagoon* was informed of our position and maintained a one mile distance between itself and the *Maersk Princess*, boxing us into a one mile stretch between the two vessels. This meant we were always within the line of sight of one of the ships. That's when we saw the other ship – it was pretty far in the distance, but when I was above the water I noticed a ship with a black hull on the horizon. It couldn't have been the *Maersk* because the *Maersk* had a burgundy hull. From our point of view, the feeling of reassurance of seeing a vessel was marred by fear. We were so small! I didn't know if they could even see us, let alone how we would be able to board either vessel.

After what felt like an eternity, Victor and I saw the *Maersk* reappearing on the horizon. *Thank god, it's found us!* I didn't know how long we had been in the water at this point. It could have been an hour, or much longer. I never felt cold but I knew I must have been because my teeth chattered involuntarily. The sea was around 17 degrees Celsius at this time of year — certainly survivable compared to other oceans — but after so long in the water, and with all the energy it was taking to stay afloat, our bodies were losing energy and heat fast. We were in a very perilous position, constantly being sucked under the water, vomiting and then going under again. We didn't speak during this time – we couldn't — we just linked arms and focused all our energies on trying to stay alive. The ship was getting closer and when it was almost upon us, two rockets shot off the back of the deck with two more rings.

'Get the ring!' I shouted to Victor.

The rings weren't next to each other so in order to get one each, we had to let go of our arms. That was a big moment. I knew that if I let go of Victor there was little chance of being able to get hold of him again, but we had no choice. We had to swim for our own survival. It was daunting, but there was no option so we just went for it. I managed to get to the ring and he grabbed one too. It was a relief to feel attached to the ship again, but doubts now assailed my mind. How are we going to get up onto this bloody thing? Nevertheless, I was dragged gradually towards the side of the ship and I was staring up at that rope ladder again.

Just get on it. Just get on it. I repeated to myself. But when I reached up to grab the bottom rung, the crew tugged on the life ring and it flew up over my head, ripping off my life jacket. The life ring slipped off me and I fell back in the water. I looked over my shoulder and Victor was at the back of the ship and his life ring was sucked through the propeller. Was that his mangled life ring? *Oh no! No NO NO!!* I didn't see Victor but I assumed he'd also gone through the propeller too. I had no life ring around me at this point and I was scraping down the side of the ship with the current. I got to the back of the ship, screaming: 'PLEASE SAVE ME! SAVE ME!' But onboard the deck of the ship I saw the first officer shaking his head and the ship disappeared again.

They can't do it. That's why he was shaking his head. Victor's dead and I can't be rescued. So that's it, then. It's over. I didn't even have a life vest over my head. The vest was still tied with straps around my back but it had been ripped off and now floated uselessly against my chest. I tried a couple of times to get it back over my head but I needed both hands to help me stay above the surface and when I tried to hook it over my head, I started sinking. The only thing I could do was keep it under my chin to keep my head out of the water. Whenever I opened my eyes, all I could see was water. I tried desperately to stay afloat but at the trough of each wave I felt myself dropping further and further into the ocean.

There's no end to this.

I'm not going to get to the bottom and push myself back up to the surface. If I sink and I can't get myself up again I'm just going to keep going down, down, down.

The floor of this ocean was a long way from the surface – over one kilometre – though by now the depth of the sea seemed irrelevant. I'd only have to sink a few metres before it was all over. I recalled how, when we were on holiday, my Grandma would tell us scary stories about drowning to keep us all away from the sea.

'It doesn't have to be deep,' she'd warn darkly. 'You can drown in a cup of tea.'

My god, how I want a cup of tea right now! I want to be on that ship, drinking a cup of tea.

But I can't because I'm drowning. It's only a matter of time before the sea claims me. The ship is gone, Victor's gone and now all my hope is gone.

I started to cry. I couldn't help it. I was utterly despondent. I was sad about Victor. A kind person and a great sailor, all he wanted was a job over the holidays. How devastating he was now gone. And I was about to join him, though my demise would be slower.

Why am I fucking crying? I scolded myself. It felt so ridiculous, alone in this great tumultuous ocean to be shedding tears but I couldn't help it. I cried for the loss of Victor. I cried for my children. I felt sorry for them all.

What is the point in shedding tears, Carolyn? How indulgent and stupid! Crying isn't going to help you, nobody can hear or see you. What am I crying for? Is this how I want to finish my life?

Then I heard a voice: 'Are you all right, Madam?'

13

I'll Not See You Today

31 December 2007, South China Sea

Victor! I'd assumed he went under the propeller but he had managed to get out of his ring just in time.

'No, I'm not bloody okay!' I started to laugh, deliriously happy to find him alive. 'Come here!'

We scrambled towards each other and, holding him, I managed to get the life jacket back over my head. But I could tell that it had ripped when the life ring came over my head because it kept deflating. So between vomiting and breathing I now had the added task of blowing into the little tube on my shoulder to keep the life jacket inflated. It was utterly exhausting but I didn't have any choice. I had to keep going.

'They'll come back for us,' I said to Victor. 'They will. They'll come back for us.'

He nodded. I'm not sure he was convinced but I knew by now they were doing everything they could to rescue us. All we had to do was hang on. Every minute in the ocean was a desperate struggle for survival. All I could taste on my lips, mouth and in my guts was salt water. And now, whenever we went under we sank further and further. *Must keep afloat, must stay above the water*, I thought as I battled against a sea that just seemed to want to drag me down to its depths. Then, after what felt like an age, I'd finally rise and break through the surface, coughing, spluttering, retching, gasping... *Breathe! Breathe! Fuck, here we go again.* And I'd be sucked under again. I kicked my legs desperately against the weight of the water but they felt entombed in concrete, the wet weather gear heavy and resistant against the waves. *How long can I keep this up?* I had no idea. I didn't feel cold at all but I knew I must be freezing because when I told Victor they were coming, my teeth chattered uncontrollably. *I must be getting hypothermic.*

When I spotted the ship for the third time, hope surged through me. *They're here. They've come back.* But the ship now stood out darkly against the fading light which meant it would soon be dusk, followed by bleak darkness. *There's not much time left. If they can't get us before we lose the light it's going to be impossible to find us again. My children are on that ship. My sons!* All I wanted at this moment was to be standing next to them, enjoying a cup of tea. That was all I wanted – to be on that ship, drinking tea. It's funny how in this time of absolute crisis, I longed to do something normal. I pictured myself up there, on that deck, clutching a steaming mug of milky tea. I was determined to make that vision a reality.

The ship seemed to be charging forward at terrific speed and from the water all we could see was the huge bow wave at the front, barrelling towards us. It was terrifying and reassuring at the same time. This ship was our only chance of getting out of the sea alive but at the same time, it was like watching a skyscraper falling on top of us in slow motion. A gigantic vessel was bearing down on us and we could do absolutely nothing to get out of its way. If Captain Sirpreet misjudged our location by just a few feet we would get sucked underneath the bow and crushed to death. I had to put all my faith in his seamanship and his crews' skills in operating this immense ship. At the point where the bow of the ship was about 30-foot away, there was absolutely no view of the bridge at all. He couldn't even see us! But we saw there were several members of the crew standing at the front of the ship who used the last of their rockets to launch three more life buoys.

One shot off into the distance, miles away from us, but two landed about ten feet from where we were treading water. Ten feet may not sound far, but when you've been tossed about in a stormy sea for hours and you are already exhausted it seems like a vast distance. We could barely swim against the large swell and with all our foul weather gear on it was an effort just to stay afloat, let alone move through the water. But we had no choice. We had to try and get to the life rings on our own. I tried to visualise myself already on that ship with a cup of tea in my hand. I had to do it. I had to let go of Victor and try to swim for my life. But my courage wavered for a moment. He was the only thing stopping me from drowning right now. If I let go of him and I didn't get the ring I would never have the energy to get him again. And with a broken life vest the chances are I would be dragged under and never come back up again. *Come on, Carolyn. You can do it.*

Victor and I looked at each other and almost at the same time, without saying a word, we detached our arms and started to swim. *Oh my god, oh my god oh my god.... Come on, come on....* I hurled myself through the water with all the energy I had left and though bobbing up and down in the swell I could see the ring getting closer and closer. It felt like I was swimming through treacle. *Come on,* I willed myself on. *Come on. Come on!*

The ring was just a couple of feet away now but all my limbs burned with pain and exhaustion. There was nothing left inside me, no energy at all. But I couldn't give up now. I had to get it. This was my only chance. I gritted my teeth and forced myself on, beyond my limits, beyond the point of exhaustion. Finally, my hand made contact with the hard life ring. *Got it!* I dragged it towards my body and slipped my head under so that it came up around my body.

A cheer erupted from the deck above me. I barely had enough energy left to lift my head but when I did, I could see people running back and forth on deck. They were cheering: 'Yes! Yes! Come on!' I was now attached to the side of the ship. *But where's Victor?* I looked over my shoulder and behind me I saw that Victor also had his life ring on. *Good. That's good. Now we both have a chance of being saved.*

My body went limp as we were pulled to the bow of the ship. For some reason I couldn't fathom why they now held us both here, at the front of the ship. My body rose and fell as the ship rolled from side to side in the waves. And every time it rolled away from me, the rope went taut and my vision was filled with the burgundy hull of the *Maersk Princess*. Then, as it rolled towards me the rope slackened and all I could see was the sky blue sides of the upper part of the ship. Time and time again I was lifted up and down in the waves...

Burgundy, blue, burgundy, blue, burgundy, blue... Meanwhile, tonnes of water cascaded over the bow, pouring over my head. *How long are they going to keep us here?*

Every time I went under the water it felt warm and calm, peaceful even. Above the surface it was all chaos and confusion, noise, crashing waves, pressure and pain on my chest. I just wanted it all to stop. Then, when I slid under the water, it did. There was a soundless tranquillity under the water. So calm, so gentle...

How are they going to do it? I wondered. We were nowhere near the rope ladder anymore, so I knew that they must have some other plan to try to get us onboard. Will they just attempt to pull us up in these rings? That would never work. If they tried that

I'd slip out of the ring and drop to my death. At some point I looked up and they were making this pushing motion at me with their palms, as if to say: 'Wait! Wait a minute.'

But what am I waiting for? I don't know. Maybe I'll just go to sleep while I wait. It's so warm here in the water, I feel I can just go to sleep and then maybe, maybe I'll see my dad.

I slipped under again and I felt the warmth flooding my body. *It's not so bad, this drowning business. It doesn't hurt, it's not painful. It's easy, like letting out a breath one has been holding onto for too long. I wish I could tell them. I wish I could let the children know that I'm okay, I'm not in any pain, that I slipped peacefully away. My children! Oh no. I won't see my children grow up.*

My heart ached with sadness. Hannah, Aaron and Joe.... I felt overcome at the thought that I would not live to see them into their adulthoods...

'Carolyn?'

A voice came to me out of the murky sea.

Dad!

'I won't see you today, Carolyn.'

You won't see me?

'No, it's not your time.'

Oh.

If it's not my time, then something has to change.

I rose to the surface again and gasped, coughing and spewing up vast quantities of sea water. I had nearly drowned! As I came to, I could hear the crew above all shouting at me and with the sound of the waves beating against the ship the noise was cacophonous. But now I could see something else. A giant cargo basket – like a big net – with a circular bottom was being slowly lowered by crane down at the middle section of the ship. The basket, the size of a large wheelie bin, dropped down behind me until it sat level in the water, still attached to the crane. *Ah, so this is how they're going to do it.*

They dragged my rope and ring over to meet the basket until I was almost level with it. All I had to do was get out of the ring and hook my fingers inside the net. I wriggled out of the ring and reached out to grasp the thick netting. But I could barely bend my fingers. They were swollen from swallowing so much water. The skin burst open at the nail beds but I barely felt a thing as I clung desperately to the netting.

I pulled myself onto the hard bottom of the basket. I just managed to get my chest in so that I was hanging half in and half out of the basket, my legs dangling over the edge into the sea. Just one more heave and I'd be inside completely. I pulled one more time and now my lower half was inside the net. *That's it! I'm in! I don't have to do anything else.*

I crouched, collapsed in a heap on the hard floor of the cargo net as the crane lifted it out of the water and it started to sway about in 42 knots of wind. Up, up, up I went, out of the sea, out of the raging ocean, away from those relentless waves. It was scary, swinging about in that small basket 30 feet in the air, remembering how the lifeboat had tipped up during its ascent to the deck. *This thing better stay upright*, I thought. But it wasn't long before the net had been raised all the way over the deck of the ship, and I saw Martin running along the deck, followed by Aaron and Joe to meet me as they lowered me down.

The look on Joe's face was horrific. He was completely white, pain and terror etched on his young features. I was alive, yes, but the look on Joe's face, seeing how traumatised he was, was too shocking to bear. *I* had done that. *I* had made my son's face look that way. The guilt was awful. When I finally hit the solid decking the relief was so overwhelming I thought I might burst into tears. They had a stretcher there waiting for me but I managed to stand up, and with the help of a couple of crew members, I staggered out of the basket. There was only one thing on my mind now.

'Please, please get Victor.' I gasped and they nodded, stepping back to allow the net to be raised and lowered into the sea again.

Martin took hold of one arm and with Aaron on my other side they led me down to the cafeteria area. The ship's medic handed me an orange thermal all-in-one and said I had to get out of my clothes and put it on. 'It's for hypothermia,' he added. Martin and a member of the crew quickly got me out of my clothes and into the thermal suit. I had little use of my limbs due to the cold and remained in the chair as they peeled off the layers. I was so happy to get out of those foul weather trousers and jacket and take off the leggings and T-shirt underneath, only now I could really feel the cold. I was shivering uncontrollably, the chill burrowing deep into my bones. The survival suit was thermal and inside there was furry black material. I pulled it on and zipped it up as quickly as my poor fingers would allow. I could feel that my digits were swollen to double their normal size and there were cracks in the skin.

'Only warm drinks and hot food,' the medic ordered.

Almost immediately I heard that Victor had been brought onto the deck with the net. *Thank God for that*. And then, wonder of wonders, somebody handed me a cup of tea! It was really the most extraordinary moment. I didn't even have to ask for it. Somebody just gave me a mug of hot, sweet milky tea and the taste of it was absolutely exquisite. This was the very moment I had visualised as I tried to save my own life. In fact, I knew that if I hadn't been rescued at that moment I may not have made it. The cold, the exhaustion, it was too much. I had hung on as long as I could and then I felt myself slipping away. But in that moment when I had nearly lost my life my Dad came to me: 'I'll not see you today, Carolyn.'

I recalled a thought that presented itself at the moment I knew

THE WATER RABBIT

I was going to live.

If I do survive, then something's got to change. My life has got to change.

I had no idea what that meant right now, there was nothing in my head beyond that vague idea: if I was given a second chance, I wasn't going to waste it. I wanted my life to be different.

14

Decompression Chamber

31 December 2007, The Maersk Princess

Everybody was in shock. Raymond wept when he saw me and said to the crew over and over again: 'Thank you for saving my wife. Thank you!'

I hadn't realised until this moment that he was injured, but now I saw there was a great big bandage over his leg. Paul, too, was in a bad way with his back, but he staggered towards me, grabbed my arm and said: 'I've done a lot of sailing over the years, but to have survived for so long in the water, it's a miracle!'

It turned out we were in the water for over four hours, which is a very long time when the water is around 17 degrees Celsius. I wore the thermal suit for a few hours, during which time I managed to warm up, helped by the hot tea and a delicious curry made by the all-Indian crew. The inside of my arms were black with bruising from being dragged around inside the life buoy, every muscle in my body ached, I had terrible diarrhoea for the first few hours after getting out of the thermal suit but apart from that, I was fine. Physically, at least.

At first the boys hardly spoke, they were so traumatised. We just hugged and held hands. Later Aaron said to me: 'I really thought I'd never see you again. I visualised a coffin full of water and I was angry at myself because my last words to you were:

'Oh, for god's sake, Mum, stop fussing.' It made me realise that they could have been my last words to you.'

My heart went out to him.

'It's okay,' I said. 'It's okay, don't be too hard on yourself. You didn't know. None of us knew.'

Truthfully, it was hard to keep pushing back the guilt myself. I couldn't believe what we had been through, how close I had come to death and how I had nearly left my children without a mother.

The message went back to the yacht club and to Hannah at home that all the crew were safe. I imagine it must have been horrific for her to have been sitting there with only minimal pieces of information occasionally filtering through via the yacht club rescue coordination. News had spread to other yacht club members of our plight but once the message went out that all crew were safe on the tanker, cheers went up and everyone felt they could enjoy the New Year.

We were to be aboard the *Maersk* for the next five days as we sailed with them to Thailand. Raymond and I were given the owner's cabin of the ship, which was very comfortable, because we had our own shower room and a small office. They filled me in on what happened when the rescue boat tipped up and how Raymond was knocked unconscious. I also saw his injuries. On his left leg, a whole lump of flesh had lifted up, the size of a burger, and he had a broken collarbone. Thankfully, the *Maersk* had a very good first aid kit, a medic and antibiotics on board. Pictures of his injuries were sent to the shore doctor who gave advice about how to treat them. If the leg got worse or became infected, the ship would have to pull into Vietnam to send him to hospital, and if this happened they would not let any of us leave with him. It was a source of worry for a while but fortunately, the crew managed to keep the wound clean and infection-free all the way to Thailand.

Our time aboard the *Maersk* acted like a decompression chamber, allowing us to recover and come to terms with what had happened, without interference from the outside world. Paul couldn't move around too much because his back was in pain; there were some books in the ship library so he lay in bed and read. Victor slept while Raymond was mostly in bed with his leg up. Meanwhile, I finally got to meet the wonderful Captain Sirpreet who filled me in on every part of the rescue from his point of view. Sitting together in the Captain's cabin, he told me that when he first heard the Pan Pan over the radio he felt very strongly that he had to respond.

'In eighteen years of sailing, I have faced every kind of challenge and sailing misadventure,' he said. 'I was even boarded by pirates one time but you know, until now I had never performed a rescue at sea. I'm planning to retire from being away at sea soon. I have three sons but with this work you're away from home for many months at a time and I don't want my sons growing up without a father at home. So I thought that if I'm going to retire, this is my last chance to perform a rescue.'

Sirpreet said there had been eight ships in the area at the time. One had already responded, telling me he was too big to help, and another was the car transporter which aided the efforts by boxing us in when we were lost at sea. Sirpreet said the other five didn't respond. That surprised me. Perhaps after the *Maersk Princess* offered to turn around, none felt compelled to join the rescue effort. Still, it seemed odd to me that they hadn't even spoken on the channel to tell us why they couldn't help. Actually, maritime law dictates that they weren't obliged to respond until the signal was upgraded to a Mayday, but still, one would think they might have a sense of moral duty to offer help.

Once the *Maersk Princess* located our position, Captain

THE WATER RABBIT

Sirpreet asked for volunteers to man the lifeboat and three men came forward: one of them an officer.

'We are all trained for emergencies like this,' said Sirpreet. 'But even so, I couldn't make anyone do this. It was very dangerous, so I had to ask my crew for volunteers. When my second-in-command volunteered I was surprised but impressed. I asked him if he was sure he wanted to go and he said *yes*. Then I explained that if he didn't go, I would go myself but that would mean he would be in charge of holding the ship steady as he was second-in-command. But all the men chose to go.'

I thought that was very brave, especially knowing that one had been injured when the boat tipped up. There were serious risks involved as the weather was so poor, and it was very humbling to know that each man aboard that lifeboat had voluntarily put himself there.

Time and again, Sirpreet had to change tactics as the weather thwarted their efforts. The rescue boat could not be used once it had tipped up and they were forced to turn around three times after losing us in the ocean. But he never once lost hope of rescuing us. He revealed that after they shot off the last three life rings, all their rescue equipment was gone.

'We'd used it all,' he sighed. 'After that we had nothing left except a life raft.'

'My god, what would you have done if we hadn't got in the rings?' I asked. It was just beginning to dawn on me how lucky we were.

'Ah, well, if that didn't work, I planned to throw the life raft over the back of the ship which I hoped you could climb into. Then I would have slowed the ship down and towed you through the night, getting you up on board the next day.'

I was silent for a moment, trying to digest this information. At that point the storm was at its worst, we had already been in the water for four hours and Victor and I were both hypothermic. I wondered how we would have coped in a life raft overnight.

Meanwhile, I found out that the wives of two of the officers were on the ship. One was the wife of the officer who had been at the back of the ship, shaking his head when I screamed out 'Save me!' She told me that he had been crying at that moment. That was why he was shaking his head. He had allowed himself to cry for a few minutes before pulling himself together. The second wife had been saying a Hindu prayer the whole time we were lost at sea, a special prayer to find people who are lost. She just kept repeating this prayer over and over again. Hearing all these accounts of the people on the ship, of what they went through during the rescue, was emotional. It made me so grateful to every single one of them. After all, who were we to them? They didn't even know us. They had no obligations towards us and yet they carried out a very dangerous, selfless operation in order to save our lives. To me, that was true heroism.

Of course, the crew of the *Maersk Princess* operated under maritime law, but Sirpreet had stepped up to help before the law obligated him to do so. He put himself and his crew in harm's way in order to save our lives. And they did it with extraordinary skill and precision. To position that ship so close to me and Victor in the water without actually killing us was amazing. If he had made a tiny mistake or misjudged the distance by just a few feet he could have been prosecuted for manslaughter. The fact that they went to such trouble to save us – that so many of them worked so hard – gave me immense faith in humanity. Every single person played a part in the rescue, even the crew in the engine room who pushed it to its absolute limits. Even the lady who prayed for four hours!

The following day, on New Year's Day 2008, there was a belated New Year's Eve Party and Captain Sirpreet called all the crew down to the big salon for a party. Then he made an amazing speech about his pride in his countrymen.

'This is the first time an all-Indian crew has sailed a *Maersk* ship,' he said. 'And now look, we have performed this very heroic, selfless act. I am so proud to be your Captain today.'

The *Maersk* had taken a big risk in turning round to get us and though the Captain had got permission to carry out the rescue, he still had to account for significant losses. They had lost 24 hours sailing time – which, in commercial sailing, represents a large amount of time and money – they had lost a great deal of fuel, they lost all their safety equipment, provisions to feed an extra seven people and both the lifeboat and the tanker itself were damaged. It amounted to a fair amount of money which they had to claim back on the insurance.

During our five days on the ship, we all gathered in the owner's cabin to write our report to the insurance company. We knew, once we got to Thailand, we'd have to give our version of the rescue, so we had to be clear about what happened, who did what and when. All of us took turns typing up the report as Raymond dictated passages from his bed. He was on a fair amount of drugs, though, and this affected his mood – none of us escaped without a sharp reprimand or barked order – so we took it in turns on the computer to get the report written. Martin, myself and the two boys also spent quite a lot of time in the captain's cabin, talking to Sirpreet. He was a very interesting man and when I spotted a dragon turtle figure on his desk I asked him what it was for.

'I'm a feng shui master,' he said. 'I really believe in it and how it helps people.'

'I know a little bit about feng shui,' I responded. 'I know the Chinese animals in the zodiac. I am a rabbit.'

'Oh, I see.'

'There are two animals in the zodiac that help each animal. As a rabbit, my helpers are sheep and pigs.'

He said: 'I'm a pig.'

At that moment a little shiver ran up my spine. For the past ten months, I had displayed a beautiful golden pig on my shelf at home. I have no idea why, but at the start of 2007, the Year of the Pig, I had decided to buy one of the little golden animals so popular in Hong Kong. This urge came totally out of the blue, and in fact, it seemed very out of character for me. Usually, I found these golden statues commemorating the start of a new lunar year not to my taste– but this pig was lovely. It was the size of a mug and for the last ten months it had sat on the shelf, glinting under the spotlight. It drew my eye every time I sat down to watch TV and several times I had found myself just staring at it, transfixed. Why? I had never bought a golden lunar animal before and yet this pig was very special to me. It all seemed strangely coincidental but when I recounted this to Sirpreet he said it wasn't a coincidence at all.

'I am a pig,' he said. 'In feng shui terms, you buying that pig and displaying it so prominently in your home brought energy to you which helped me to find you, as a pig to a rabbit.'

It was funny. The other extraordinary coincidence was that my friend Reine who stayed with Hannah during the crisis was a sheep, my other helper animal! So I had a sheep and a pig helping me. But Sirpreet told me we all also have a secret helper animal. He told me as a rabbit, mine was a dog. He explained the secret helper would be something like if you get a flat tyre on your car and then someone stops to help you change the wheel. They would likely be a dog and I'd not know it, just a person who helps in a quiet way or a way you don't really realise. I had no idea if I even knew any people who were dogs in the Chinese astrological cycle, so I didn't give it much more thought.

It was only much later that I discovered Roger, who coordinated the rescue communication from the yacht club and kept Hannah informed as much as possible, was a Chinese dog.

Our time on board the *Maersk* was mostly quiet and contemplative. Every now and then we could send an email, but apart from that we were cut off from the outside world. We talked, slept and read, each of us coming to terms with what had happened, examining our lives and the impact the disaster had had on us. Aaron said that he didn't want to go back to London, he didn't like the course he was studying at university and didn't feel happy on campus either. Raymond wasn't prepared to entertain the idea of Aaron dropping his degree after just one term but I understood that, like for all of us, coming close to death had affected Aaron deeply. You don't realise just how precious life is until you come close to losing it, and that had sparked in all of us the feeling that we didn't want to waste our lives doing things we didn't like. I understood where he was coming from, of course, but I wasn't sure he had hit on the right solution.

'Look, you can't change the course right now so why not stick it out until the summer?' I suggested. 'Then, if you've done the year and you still want to change you can reapply for something else. By then, the choices for the second year might be more in line with what you want to do.'

He agreed to think about it. Meanwhile, I had my own thinking to do. I was coming to terms with the momentous decision I had made while drowning. And the thought of what might come next was overwhelming.

One afternoon, I was sitting at the desk in the cabin while Raymond slept on the bed and the tears simply wouldn't stop. Normally, I wouldn't cry in front of Raymond. I was used to putting a brave face on, but now he was sleeping and I was so distraught, it felt like the world was ending. At that moment the medic came in to check on Raymond and found me sitting there, weeping silently into my cupped hands. I didn't even know what for. Perhaps it was shock, perhaps it was the trauma of what I had been through but I was swept up in sadness and I couldn't stop crying. The medic didn't say anything to me. He seemed to acknowledge the pain and simply looked away as though to say: 'It's okay.' There was compassion in his face, empathy. He didn't intrude or ask what was wrong, he didn't want to interfere, he just looked away and went to see to Raymond's leg. I was tired, I was confused. I was faced with the enormity of the promise I'd made myself, that I was going to change my life, and I knew there was going to be a huge cost to doing that.

At this point very little came to me in clear, well-formed thoughts. The only certainty I had was that I was done with sailing. *Purple X* was gone and with it my desire to step onboard another yacht. I certainly didn't want to sail round the world anymore. But my other thoughts were vaguer and more ephemeral, cascading one on top of another like a waterfall. It was hard to form a coherent idea from the tumbling, churning turmoil inside but this was what I knew: I had been unhappy and I knew I could be happier. Things could be better somehow. I had been given the gift of life and I didn't want to waste it.

There would be consequences to this decision but then... I had saved myself! I was a capable person, so I could survive other things. I could survive making difficult decisions. If I had been saved from death there had to be a reason and I had to make that reason count for something.

I don't ever want to be depressed again.

I don't want to be thinking, when my time finally comes, that I regret anything.

If I can be responsible for hauling myself back on that ship when I am minutes from death, then I can damn well live a life that is meaningful

THE WATER RABBIT

to me.

I've been a wife, and a mother but what is the point of anything unless I can be happy?

What am I doing?

What is my life's purpose?

These were the questions that assailed me as we crossed the ocean towards Thailand. Physically, I was well, but inside, I was in pieces. Something very fundamental had changed for me. In those few seconds between life and death there had been a paradigm shift and I knew that once we reached land, my life would never be the same again.

15

EVERYTHING'S A MESS

5 January 2008, Thailand

PULLING INTO MAP Ta Phut port in Thailand from the deck of a tanker was an amazing experience. I had watched these large ships manoeuvring into port from the shore, but being aboard one was very different. From my special vantage point, I could appreciate the captain's skill in moving the enormous vessel. How could he be so precise when he couldn't even see the end of the tanker, I marveled. Then, once we were safely docked, we had one final get-together.

The crew had made a sign to commemorate the rescue which read *Maersk Princess & Purple X Rescue Mission 31 December 2007* and we all stood in the photo on deck with the sign. It felt like a very significant moment and an important record of the event. The people in this photo had gone out of their way to save our lives and to me, they represented the very best qualities of humanity. I hoped that they would all be recognised and rewarded for their heroism. We said emotional goodbyes, exchanged email addresses and then it was time to disembark.

Reality started creeping back into our lives. During those five days onboard the *Maersk*, we had been cocooned from the world and the consequences of the disaster, but no more. Before we could even disembark, a man from the insurance company boarded the ship to talk to us and brief us on what would happen next. Then, immigration arrived, and we were all interrogated on what had happened and why we were entering Thailand. Before we could even step onto dry land again we were faced with a barrage of questions. It was frustrating, especially as I knew that Hannah and Reine were in the port, ready to meet us off the ship. Finally, we were allowed to step down the gangplank, walk through the security gates and into the port terminal. Both Raymond and Paul were wheeled down on wheelchairs and there was an ambulance waiting to take them to the hospital. I spotted Hannah straight away on the other side of the barriers, watching as her father was wheeled down the gangplank and then loaded into the back of an ambulance.

She looked distressed. After everything she had been through she was now watching her dad being taken to hospital. The rest of us looked perfectly okay, just walking off the ship, but Hannah was distracted by the sight of her dad inside the ambulance. The ambulance doors were shutting and my daughter was alarmed.

'Aren't you going with him to the hospital?' she asked me sharply.

'We're not allowed,' I replied. 'He needs an operation on his leg and he's going straight into surgery. They say we can't go with him.'

I had imagined this moment many times while we were aboard the *Maersk*, visualising how Hannah and I would run into each other's arms, crying with relief, and hug each other tightly. But nothing like that happened. In fact, the reunion felt awkward and difficult. Of course I was delighted to see her, but she seemed preoccupied, watching Raymond being taken away by ambulance.

The rest of us were loaded into a minivan for the two-hour drive to Bangkok where Raymond's company had arranged rooms for us at the Shangri-La hotel. I sensed during that journey that Hannah was angry with me and I couldn't help feeling terrible about it. Terrible that we'd put her through this. We'd inflicted so much worry on everybody. My poor daughter! Thank God she wasn't on the yacht when the disaster happened. It was a blessing. Yet, at the same time, she had no idea what we had all been through and that separated her from us. *Did she know how close I had come to dying? Had anyone told her?* Similarly, we didn't know the trauma she had suffered, stuck in Hong Kong on her own, not knowing what was going on. It must have been extremely stressful for her. *We need to sit down and talk properly.* I wanted to share our experiences together... But that never happened. In fact, I wasn't at all prepared for what happened next...

At the hotel, Hannah took control of the check in.

'I'll do it,' she announced.

'Well, I've got my passport,' I started.

'No, I'll do it...' she said again, more firmly this time.

I think she was trying to be useful by stepping into her father's role and taking charge. I imagine during those hours we were lost at sea she must have felt very helpless, but I didn't like it. She was twenty years old and I was forty-four. I'd just helped coordinate a life-and-death rescue, for goodness' sake, and was more than capable of checking into a hotel! But I didn't make a fuss. It really wasn't important. *Just let her do what she needs to do.*

So she organised us all into rooms and allocated me a room with Joe. I must admit it felt strange to be checking into a plush hotel wearing the grubby T-shirt and leggings I had on when I was rescued. Over my shoulder I still carried the bright yellow Grab Bag with the words *SOS Grab Bag* emblazoned along the side. Fortunately, Hannah had brought us some clothes from home, so once in the room I changed into fresh clothes. Later, the meagre belongings that had been rescued from the yacht arrived on a trolley in black bin bags. We had to make a quick dash across the road to a luggage shop to buy some cheap bags to take our stuff back to Hong Kong because we couldn't very well travel with black bin liners!

I called the hospital and spoke to Raymond. He said he was about to go into surgery so there was nothing more for us to do tonight and no point coming to see him. Paul, meanwhile, had had an X-ray which revealed the bone above his coccyx was fractured, but they couldn't do anything to fix it so he returned to the hotel.

Once we'd all settled into our rooms, the group met again at the poolside restaurant. There was nothing more to be done and to be honest, I was ready for a stiff drink so I ordered a gin and tonic while a few others ordered beers. This was to be the first alcohol to pass my lips since leaving the Philippines, but Hannah disapproved.

'How can you sit there drinking bloody cocktails?' she asked, incredulous.

'Well, why not?' said Aaron.

'Dad's in hospital!' she shot back.

'Dad's fine, he just needs an operation on his leg.'

'Well, I think it's disgraceful!'

She turned to me: 'What kind of wife are you?'

'I just spoke to your dad,' I tried to reassure her. 'He said to sit back and relax because there's nothing to be done.'

Martin added: 'You know, Hannah, it was your mum who nearly died. I think she can have one drink...'

The problem was that Hannah had no clue of what I'd been through, and I looked fine. Perhaps if she had known she wouldn't have been so judgemental of me. Perhaps not – there was something more to her anger than mere disgust, something deeper and unspoken. She seemed suspicious of me.

'So when are you going to go and see Dad in hospital?' she asked.

'When I can,' I said. 'When he's out of surgery and the doctors say it's okay. What else can I do?'

This wasn't enough for Hannah. She kept haranguing me, accusing me of being an uncaring wife and in the end, I was so upset I abandoned my gin and tonic and went back up to the room.

I changed into my pyjamas and put myself to bed, crying quietly into my pillow. Nothing felt right, our lives were in turmoil. I tried to sleep but it was impossible. Later that evening there was a gentle knock on the door.

'I've come to see if you're okay,' Martin said.

'Thanks, I'm fine. Where is everybody?'

'They're all going to bed and Hannah took a tuk-tuk to the hospital. Where's Joe? Isn't he sharing a room with you?'

'I don't know where he's gone. I don't know where anybody is! I don't know what room numbers they're in because Hannah did the check in.'

'But you're not meant to be left on your own. The doctor said that because of the PTSD, you shouldn't be alone.'

We'd had a discussion with the on-shore doctor of the *Maersk* before disembarking and he had explained that people with PTSD may fear abandonment, so shouldn't be left alone in the immediate aftermath of the trauma. He'd explained that having other people around would help alleviate flashbacks and intense anxiety.

At that moment Hannah returned from the hospital. She came into the room and found me and Martin sat on the bed, chatting. Her mood had not improved since visiting her father.

'Where's Joe?' I asked her. 'Isn't he meant to be in my room?'

'Well, you've got Martin, haven't you?' she sneered.

'What's that meant to mean?'

'Dad's dying in hospital and all you care about is chatting to Martin!' she exploded.

'Hannah!' I exclaimed. I was really upset by what she was saying.

Now Martin intervened: 'Your mum's not meant to be left on her own. She has PTSD.'

'Well, she's got you, hasn't she?' she countered.

'No, I'm sharing a room with Aaron.'

Now Hannah threw some Thai baht on the bed and stormed off, shouting: 'If you even care, Dad's in hospital.'

Martin left to go to sleep in the room he was sharing with Aaron. I found out later that Joe had put himself to sleep in Paul's room. Victor too had gone to sleep on the sofa in Paul's room. Hannah was with Reine and according to my friend she was up all night, distressed by the whole situation. She told her that I seemed not to care about my husband. She clearly saw, more clearly than I, something that I had spent a long time trying to avoid, something which I didn't want to acknowledge.

That night, alone once again, I began to face an unhappy realisation: that in order to make myself happy, I had to leave Raymond. It wasn't an easy thought and one I didn't want to give too much space in my head to, knowing that he was in hospital at this very moment. The worst thing was that I had no idea about how this would impact the whole family. If Hannah's reaction was anything to go by, the next few months were going to be horrendous. But my daughter wasn't blind or insensitive. She must have known for a very long time that I wasn't happily married, and whatever her judgement right now about my behaviour towards her dad, I deserved more than I was getting in this relationship. Martin was showing care and concern way beyond anything Raymond had done and though we were just friends, she clearly resented the way he treated me. How sad and confusing for her!

It was the first night I had been on dry land in weeks and yet, I barely slept a wink. Every time I managed to nod off for a few minutes, I'd wake with a start, wondering where I was. Then my mind would go back to the same tormented state: *What am I going to do? Where do I go from here?*

The next morning Aaron and Martin came to my room and I ordered breakfast to be brought up. I needed to eat but couldn't face going down to the buffet. I felt sick to my stomach about the whole situation. This was rather unexpected, after all we were all safe and in a good hotel. Our flights back to Hong Kong and Victor's back to Manila were all arranged for later in the day. Half an hour later Hannah joined us.

'What's going on?' she asked.

'I've just ordered breakfast,' I said. 'I can't face going downstairs.'

'Oh really? You can't face going down for a breakfast that's included in the room? So now you're going to charge Dad's credit card for breakfast?'

What on earth was she going on about?

'Hannah, it's not just your Dad's money,' I had to set her straight. 'I am part of this marriage. The only reason we have so much money is because I've literally sacrificed my whole life for this family. And if I want bloody poached eggs brought to my room after I nearly died, I'll damn well have them!'

'You need to grow up!' she shouted at me.

'Hannah, you need to calm down,' Aaron jumped in. 'You weren't there, you don't know how bad it was.'

That didn't help. It only served to diminish her own distress and enrage her further. She said I should show more care for her father.

When she stopped Martin, who had been sitting there quietly the whole time, said: 'You might want to take a minute and look in the mirror.' Then he walked out the room.

'WHAT'S IT GOT TO DO WITH YOU?' she screamed after him. 'YOU'RE NOT EVEN PART OF THIS FAMILY!'

The whole scene was dreadful. It seemed like surviving the disaster had been the easy part, now I had to survive the shipwreck of my life. Everything now seemed such an impossible mess: my marriage, my life, the paperwork and on top of that my daughter hated me... *Where will all this end? Where will we be in six months' time? Christ, I don't even know if I can get through another six minutes of this!*

Later that morning I went downstairs to fetch a tuk tuk to the hospital and found Hannah curled up in a corner, reading her book. None of our group were talking to her after her outbursts – everyone was giving her a bit of 'space', but I felt only compassion for my daughter, and tremendous sadness. *She's confused, she's angry....* It was heart-breaking. I went to speak to her.

'Look, come on Hannah.. it's all been very...'

'Don't talk to me! It's ridiculous. You won't even go to see Dad.'

'I'm going now! I need to get some Thai baht...'

'Fine!'

When I arrived at the hospital with Joe and Aaron, Raymond was out of surgery and in a private room watching *Dead Calm*, a nautical thriller starring Nicole Kidman. I vaguely recalled watching it a few years earlier.

'Doesn't the yacht sink in this movie?' I asked. Raymond nodded. 'Well, what are you watching this for? Didn't we just live through this whole film!' I asked, agog.

'It's something to watch,' he shrugged.

I was pleased to see him awake and seemingly well after his operation. Raymond said the surgery had been successful but the doctors told him he needed to stay in hospital for another week to recover. But I was keen to return to Hong Kong so we could get Aaron back to university and Joe back to school. Then there was all the paperwork for the yacht to sort out.

'You've been through a lot, Carolyn,' Raymond said. 'Why don't you book into one of these fancy five-star resorts in Thailand for a week? Stay in a spa and then we can travel back together.'

'I can't do that,' I said. 'I've got to sort the boys out. I can't just drop everything and stay in a spa resort.'

'Why not?'

'No, I'm not going to do that. Raymond, there's a lot to sort out.'

I could never have contemplated being pampered whilst my kids were struggling. Besides, I wanted to speak to him properly. There had been no talking over the past few years of how his job had taken its toll on us all in various ways. Was now the right time? I didn't know. Would there ever be a good time to address our issues?

'Raymond,' I started. 'Er...you know that everything's a mess at the moment. I'm not happy. Something's got to change. I ... erm.. I'll probably want to be on my own for a bit.'

'Hmmm....'

I don't think he heard or understood what I meant. I wasn't even sure myself. All I knew was that something was very wrong. *Perhaps now isn't the right time. Let's just get over this next hurdle and get back to Hong Kong. Then we can talk properly.*

Back at the hotel we prepared to fly back. Hannah was going on a ski trip to France with her university friends and wasn't due to fly till later that day. It was a difficult farewell at the poolside restaurant.

'Hannah, we're going to the airport now,' I started.

'Yeah, okay, whatever.... I'm going to see Dad this afternoon.' she said pointedly.

'I understand you're not happy, Hannah, but I've got to get back to Hong Kong. Your father suggested I stay in a spa hotel for the next week, but I can't do that. I'm going to get your brothers back to school and university and sort all this shit out.'

'Yeah, fine,' she said, airily.

At the airport we discovered the check-in queues were massive. I decided to call Hannah to warn her.

'Make sure you allow plenty of time to get your flight because it's a really long queue,' I said.

'Mum! I don't need you to tell me how to get around.'

'Okay, but we're not used to leaving Bangkok and it's a really long queue.'

One last fight before our flight! It was all so miserable. After we finally managed to check in, I took myself off to the airport bar for a large gin and tonic. My nerves were in shreds, my life in tatters. The thing was, Hannah could see there was something wrong. She was no fool and whatever her emotional reaction I had to admit that I did feel detached from the marriage and she could see that. However unpleasant her behaviour, she clearly had a fairly accurate analysis of the situation. Reine and Martin joined me at the bar.

Reine joked: 'They might have taught you a lot in the forces, Martin, but being mates with Carolyn is pretty fucking stressful!'

I got on the plane, carrying the Grab Bag as hand luggage, looking for all the world like a very nervous passenger, ready with her emergency bag to bolt at any minute. My seat was next to the boys for the three hour flight but Reine offered to swap.

'I think you should sit next to Martin,' she whispered. 'I think it would be good for you to talk to another adult. It was all very distressing, the way Hannah was carrying on.'

I agreed and once my seat belt was buckled, unfurled my free copy of the *South China Morning Post*. "Sailing Holiday Turns Into Ocean Nightmare," read the headline of the top story on the front page. I scanned the opening paragraphs:

> 'What began as a sunny Christmas sailing holiday in the Philippines ended with a dramatic New Year's Eve sea rescue for a Hong Kong family and the crew of their yacht. Carolyn and Raymond Lee, along with their sons Aaron, 18, and Joe, 16, and three crew members were sailing home from the Philippines when disaster struck the *Purple X*, their 49-foot Oyster yacht....'

Oh god! I quickly closed the paper and stashed it away in the pocket of the seat in front of me. I didn't need to read anymore. Once we took off, Martin got us both a drink and we started to talk about the situation with Hannah. I was very upset about it all, but Martin reassured me, insisting she would calm down eventually.

'I'm worried about *you*,' he said.

The truth of the matter was, through the trauma, inevitably we had become closer. His military background proved its worth. He had mucked in with all the laundry on the Maersk, checking up on the boys and me. I was not used to this, I was used to being the one to organise things. I was used to being the carer and not being cared for.

'Martin, I don't know what's going on,' I started. 'I can't think straight.'

'I know, I know. It's understandable and I don't want to put any pressure on you. None at all. I just want you to know I'm here for you. The thing is, I knew how close you were to dying in those last ten minutes. I could see it. I could see you were slipping away and all I wanted at that moment was to jump into the sea. It was obvious you were in peril.'

'But you would have drowned!'

'I didn't do it, did I? I'm just trying to let you know how I feel. I didn't even know myself until that moment. I thought about jumping in because I didn't want you to die alone.'

Suddenly, I was furious.

'But you've got a six year old daughter!'

'Like I said, I didn't do it, Carolyn. I just felt I couldn't let you die on your own. And now that you're here… Well, I have to tell you how I feel. I don't want to put any pressure on you. This is your life, you have to decide what you want and I know that won't be easy, but please know this: I will wait. However long it takes I'll wait for you.'

It was all too much. I didn't know what to think or feel. I liked Martin, I liked the solidity of him. He was kind, caring, calm, trustworthy and honourable. Solid. Yes, it was true, I wasn't happy in my marriage, but I didn't know if I saw a future with him either. I couldn't deal with this at the moment – it was too much. Hannah's distress was heart-breaking enough. I couldn't cope with Martin's feelings as well. Besides, after twenty-two years of marriage, I wasn't going to jump from one relationship to another. Ironically, despite many years of loneliness, the one thing I knew for certain right now was that I needed to be on my own.

16

Martin

Friday 19 October 2007 – The White Stag Pub, Wan Chai, Hong Kong

'What have you got on your face?'
'Is it a bird?'
'Are those feathers?'
The lads at the bar were curious about the extraordinary face paint shimmering on my face, neck and towards my chest. *The bird of paradise!* I'd forgotten it was even there. I'd come out to Wan Chai to meet Derek, my friend Marian's husband who was in town for a few days. Marian and I had become very close during our early years in Hong Kong, but she and Derek had been living back in Yorkshire for some time now, so I made a point of seeing Derek whenever he was out here on business. The face painting was a favour for a friend. I was alone again and staring down the barrel of a five-day weekend, thanks to the public holidays. Raymond was in Shanghai on business, Joe was camping with his mates, so I offered myself as a canvas for my friend's wife Catriona. She was a highly skilled face paint artist and this year entering a UK competition with the theme 'Wild and Tropical'. It felt like a better way to spend my weekend than just being on my own. After all, most of my friends were going to be away and there were very few people to hang out with.

THE WATER RABBIT

I'd invited Catriona over for the day on Friday and before lunch she set about painting a tropical frog sitting across the bridge of my nose and cheek. For the last effort of the day, she wanted to paint an exotic bird of paradise in bright fuchsia and gold that rose up from my forehead and whose extravagant plumage flowed down my neck and onto the top of my chest. It really was an amazing piece of artwork but it took quite a long time and after she'd put the finishing touches to it and photographed me for the competition, I was running late and still needed to walk the dog.

'Well, I see you haven't changed, Carolyn!' Derek laughed when he set eyes on me. I'd gone to meet him with the full bird of paradise still plastered over my face, neck and chest.

'What? Have I gone a bit over the top with my make up?' I joked.

Back in the day I enjoyed dressing up and wearing fanciful costumes at Halloween so I knew Derek would find this funny. We had a good catch up at the Foreign Correspondents' Club before moving onto the White Stag where Derek was due to meet a couple of other friends and watch the Rugby World Cup match. That's when we got chatting to another group of Brits who seemed fascinated by my face painting. They started asking questions about the bird of paradise, though by this point I'd completely forgotten it was there. One of them was a fellow called Martin.

Martin was out in Hong Kong for a short-term contract in the security business. He had got the gig through a former army contact and the group had been booked to work at a major golfing tournament. Martin was friendly, down-to-earth and easy to talk to. But when I asked him if he had his visa to enter China he seemed surprised.

'Oh, I was told I don't need one and Hong Kong was part of

China now.'

'No, you need a visa to visit the mainland,' I said.

He looked worried.

'I'm meant to be flying to Shanghai tomorrow to start this job.'

'Okay, don't worry. I know a good agent who can process visas quickly, even during the holidays. I can take you there tomorrow. We'll get it all sorted.'

Martin was very grateful for my help and the next day I took him to the travel agency. Afterwards, as a thank you, he took me out to lunch.

It was interesting to find out about Martin. We were the same age and he had been stationed in Hong Kong from 1988 to 1990 during his army years but hadn't been back since so he was fascinated to see how much Hong Kong had changed. Born in Guildford, he'd grown up in Cornwall but moved around with the army. When he met his wife they had settled down in Hampshire and had a little girl together. Sadly, the relationship hadn't worked and now they were divorcing. To me, Martin seemed like a really decent, modest guy. There was nothing flashy about him at all; he was funny, friendly and very grateful for my help in sorting out his visa. I was always keen to make new friends. Hong Kong could be a difficult place to live when so many travellers were just passing through. I got used to making friends quickly and, after so many years away from the UK, I was also fascinated to know what was going on in my home country. What news did they have on the government, the economic situation and societal changes? I'd started to hanker for some elements of life in the UK like the British countryside, which held a strong place in my heart due to my childhood in Lymm. I sought the companionship of those I could relate to. And Martin certainly seemed like good company.

THE WATER RABBIT

After his stint at the golfing tournament in Shanghai, Martin's friend found him more work in China and Hong Kong, and he was back and forth quite a bit from the UK. We met a couple more times and messaged frequently over the next few weeks. When I asked what he was doing for Christmas, he replied: 'I don't know, to be honest. There's not much to go back to the UK for. My ex will have my daughter. It's all a bit miserable, really.'

'Why don't you come with us on the yacht to the Philippines?' I suggested. 'You can be our eighth crew member. We could do with another pair of hands.'

'My sailing might be a bit rusty.'

'That's okay. We can take you out on the yacht before we go, give you a little briefing.'

'Okay, sounds good,' Martin agreed.

So a few weeks before we left, Raymond and I took Martin out on the yacht to show him the ropes. Martin had sailed round the Isle of Wight when he was in the army, but it had been a long time since he'd crewed and his level of sailing was not on a par with ours. It didn't matter. As a capable, physically strong man who could follow instructions, I knew he would be a perfectly good member of our crew. Raymond too was happy enough to take another person aboard as we needed the extra help and he was keen to have Martin's security experience in case of any issues with people trying to board the yacht. I introduced them when Martin came round to the houseboat for lunch and they seemed to get on well from the start. It wasn't unusual for either of us to make new friends on golfing or sailing weekends, especially if they came from the UK. But as it turned out, the practice trip on the yacht was a total disaster.

Purple X had been in the boatyard at the Royal Hong Kong Yacht Club for several days, having a fair amount of maintenance work done on it. Now the three of us, joined by Joe and his school mate, took her out of the marina for a very basic lesson in operating the yacht. Raymond was instructing Martin on how to put the mainsail up while I was on the helm. But five minutes in, the topping lift that holds the boom in place slipped its clutch and hit me on the head.

'Owww!' I cried out.

'Jesus Christ!' Raymond exploded. 'What the hell? We've just had the boat back from the yard. This is unacceptable boat maintenance.'

I clutched my throbbing head.

'Carolyn! Call him, would you?' Raymond snapped.

'Raymond, can't you do it?' I said quietly. 'I think I've got a concussion.'

'You're the one in charge of boat maintenance...' he shot back.

A heavy silence fell between us.

Martin spoke up.

'I think that was a pretty bad crack on the head,' he said to Raymond. 'I've had less serious injuries playing rugby and been taken off the pitch. Carolyn, are you okay?'

'Erm, not really,' I groaned.

Of course, I was used to the way Raymond treated me, but having Martin there, showing genuine concern, was embarrassing. I could see Martin was both upset at my injury and disturbed by Raymond's apparent lack of concern. As for me, I felt ashamed of Raymond's behaviour and our apparent inadequacies as a couple. I didn't want to draw attention to them any further by causing a scene, so after about twenty minutes or so, I called Roger, the boatyard manager at the yacht club. It was an awkward call, as I felt a bit rough and Roger was in the middle of another job, his head down the bilge of a yacht in the yard. He wondered what he was supposed to do about it at that moment. I was thinking the same, but I felt I had to call as Raymond was so

THE WATER RABBIT

mad about it. We resolved that the boat would be returned to the yard to have things sorted and everything calmed down.

I really was injured, so we motored back to the berth to assess the situation, calling Melinda to come over from the houseboat with ice for my head. Eventually, feeling a bit better, we set out again and this time I took a back seat as we did a couple of hours light cruising around so Martin could get the idea.

I brushed off the incident, like so many others with Raymond. But the more time Martin spent in our company, the more he saw the disharmony in our marriage. Raymond wanted things to be done well. His standards were very high; this was, after all, how he'd been so successful in his career. But the relentless pressure of his job had spilled over to his personal life. I couldn't hide it, it was obvious to anyone who spent time with us and especially on the boat, that Raymond gave orders as if I was on the payroll. Wanting to keep the peace, and also wanting things done well, I felt obliged to work hard to get everything sorted. I just never felt appreciated for doing any of them and was often the one who copped it if things weren't as they should be. After all, I was not the one working sixteen-hour days so I felt I had to 'earn my keep'.

At the point we went away to the Philippines, Martin was just a friend, nothing more, albeit one I found easy to talk to and confide in. He shared with me the details of his marriage breakdown and I was curious to learn more about what led to the divorce. How had he come to that life-changing decision when his daughter was only six years old? What impact did he think it would have on his relationship with her? How much would he see her if he moved out to Hong Kong?

I asked because I was genuinely interested in Martin's situation, but I was also curious for myself. I knew I was unhappy in my marriage but I always feared the consequences of leaving Raymond so much I never seriously considered it. Not until, that is, I nearly died. Then, Martin's 'confession' took me totally by surprise. I never imagined that his feelings for me were so serious. Now here he was, changed as we all were by our experiences, determined not to let life pass him by, attempting to live his own authentic life. But to be honest, I couldn't cope with it. His love for me was just one more thing for me to deal with, and right now, I didn't feel I could cope with anything.

I was so grateful when my brother Andrew landed in Hong Kong the day after we got back. He had been distressed to learn how close I had come to death and insisted on flying out to help me get back on my feet. It was so reassuring to have Andrew with us. I didn't ask for him to come, he just did it. As my twin we shared a bond and he knew I needed him at this moment. Once Andrew arrived, Martin also stayed on the houseboat to help. The first job was to get Aaron back to university. He was still hesitant about returning to the UK and was probably still suffering from shock after the accident, but he agreed to finish the first year, after which he could re-evaluate his options. Joe, on the other hand, wanted to return to school straight away. Martin was used to dealing with practical things and was more than happy to help ferry Joe to school and take Aaron to buy a new laptop before he returned to university.

Meanwhile, I started on all the paperwork, trying to get things in order. My life was busy in normal times, but the post-accident fall out had created a list of urgent items that needed immediate attention, not easy when I was dealing with my own PTSD. It felt good to have both men in the house during this time. Joe and Aaron both liked Martin and my brother. Andrew's arrival gave some sense of normality and stability to the boys, and they appreciated his humour and ability to make things feel lighter and easier. It also helped that Andrew and Martin hit it off from the start, allowing me to take a breath. Martin may have had feelings for me, but I put this to the back of my mind as I focused on getting the boys sorted out. They were my priority right now.

During this time, I was in communication with the hospital in Thailand about Raymond's wounds. The first operation had only been partially successful so he needed a second. I also needed to fill out tons of forms and documents for the insurance company to account for our missing vessel. It was exhausting and I felt overwhelmed and panicky a lot of the time. I was so stressed I couldn't sleep properly at night so I bought some over-the-counter sleeping pills just to give my mind a little rest at night. There was too much to think about and I didn't even know where to start.

Martin stayed with us a few days and my brother was around for a week before returning to the UK. Then, a week after our return, on 13 January, I went to collect Raymond from the airport. He was wheeled into the Arrivals lounge in a wheelchair, looking frail and vulnerable, and the moment I saw him, I burst into tears.

'Why are you crying?' he asked, confused.

'I..I...I don't know...' I sniffed. 'I'm exhausted, I'm worried about you, your leg. It's all just too much.' It was true that I was worried about Raymond, but it was more than that. It was everything. I was a mess, worried about the future, unable to think straight or keep it together.

My anxiety threatened to overwhelm me all the time. I kept telling myself I'd been through bad situations before so I could weather this particular storm but it really felt as if I was on the verge of losing everything I'd worked so hard for over the years. I was at a crossroads and the idea of giving up my marriage and everything stable in my life was terrifying. *How can I let it all go?*

At night my mind raced: *Carolyn, you can get through this. Yes, you can. But what about the boys? They are still traumatised by the whole experience – is it fair to do this to them now? Joe won't talk about the accident. Aaron doesn't want to go back to university. I have to make these choices and I don't know where the support is going to come from. Martin says he'll be there for me, but I don't even know if I want him either. No, I have to do this on my own. I have to take responsibility for my future and everyone else is going to have to go with it. As long as I don't lose my kids. Please God don't let me lose my kids! What can I do? What can I do? I've stayed too long as it is...*

In the days before Raymond returned, I was really struggling. By the time he returned from Thailand, my mind was made up and I told him 'I can't go on like this.'

He frowned. He could see I was not myself. I was in a bit of a state.

'You don't have to worry, Carolyn. I'll deal with all the paperwork.' he said.

'Yes, but it's not just that, is it? It's not just the paperwork, it's everything. I'm not happy. I just want everything to go away. I need some time to think, to be on my own. I can't think straight.'

'Hmm... okay, I can see you're distressed,' Raymond said. 'But you're a strong person. You'll get through this. It will pass.'

Raymond thought a holiday might do us good, so we went away in early February for Chinese New Year to a spa resort in Chiang Mai, Thailand. Joe came too, but it was no good. I simply didn't want to be with Raymond anymore. It all came to a head and I finally told him that I couldn't do it anymore, I wanted to be on my own. He vacillated between anger and appeasement – one minute telling me how wicked I was for breaking up the family and the next trying to reassure me that we would be okay. I appreciated his efforts, but the truth was, I just didn't want to be there. A five star wellness retreat wasn't going to fix anything.

'No, it won't be okay,' I said. 'That ship has literally sailed. I'm done. I'm exhausted.'

THE WATER RABBIT

'How can you do this to your family? How can you send your son off to university knowing he's leaving a broken family?'

There was no point arguing any more — whatever I said, he wasn't going to like the answer. When he asked Joe to beg me to stay, our son refused.

'You can't keep somebody that doesn't want to stay,' he said simply.

It was a disastrous trip but at least it demonstrated to us both that our relationship was at its end. When we got home I suggested I move out and he agreed.

'Okay, I accept your decision,' he said finally. Together, we found a small apartment and he offered to pay the rent for six months. After that, we would reassess the situation. At the age of forty-five, and just weeks after our trip to the Philippines, I was about to leave my old life behind and start all over again on my own. I had no idea what was coming next but at least the decision was made. It had been an agonising choice, and one I didn't take lightly, knowing that I would be leaving my youngest son at home. But in some ways I felt more peaceful. Joe understood the situation – he knew I wasn't happy and he accepted I wanted to leave. I had been given a second chance at life and I wasn't going to waste it.

17

ALONE

February 2008, Hong Kong

THE DAY BEFORE I was due to move off the houseboat, alone I packed a few belongings into boxes. I didn't want to take much – after all, the apartment was tiny so I couldn't fit a lot in – but I needed the basics like plates, cutlery, chairs to sit on and a few pieces of furniture. How would remain on the houseboat, his home. He wandered through to where I was packing

'Don't take everything, Mum!' he exclaimed, half-joking, half-serious.

Melinda, our home help, looked at him with compassion: 'Don't worry, Joe. Your mum isn't taking much. And we have so many things.'

But his words cut me. I didn't want to be doing this, breaking up Joe's home, and the thought of how much this might be hurting him was upsetting. Perhaps for Joe, the idea of my leaving hadn't felt real until now. After all, Raymond and I had slept in the same bed the whole time.

Joe was the one most directly affected by our separation and as much as this would be hard for him, I knew from our discussions in Thailand that he wanted me to be happy. The other two were at university in the UK so we told them during a family conference call. Aaron didn't seem too surprised. Hannah was angry, but I think that came from knowing things had not been great for a long time. Later she acknowledged that she couldn't remember a time when me and Raymond were happy together. For now, we didn't talk about divorce, we only said that I was moving out to have some time alone. As for Joe, I reassured him that I would always be there for him, no matter what. Joe was a perceptive boy. He knew something was wrong and even said to me: 'You know, Mum, when we were all on that yacht, in that situation, we had to work together to save ourselves, but now that we're home on dry land, we all survive in our own way.'

I found that very wise. And he was right. We each had to find our own way through. For him, it was a matter of putting the accident behind him. He didn't want to talk about it to anyone. His friends worried that he was burying his emotions, bottling up the trauma, but I knew that Joe was handling things in his own way. He wasn't an extrovert like his sister, he didn't wear his emotions on his sleeve, but he was thoughtful and sensitive. And if this was how he wanted to handle things, we had to respect that.

'If he doesn't want to talk, just let him be,' I advised his friends. 'He'll open up when he's ready.'

The actual day of the move a couple of weeks later was awful. I had spent my whole married life working to build a comfortable, loving home for us and our children. The irony now was that I was leaving it. What was really sickening to me was that my mother had happily walked away from my childhood home and here I was, feeling this was the hardest thing in the world. I stood in the shower that morning and wept. I had never imagined it would come to this. When I'd taken my marriage vows with Raymond all those years ago, I thought they were for life. Since then, I had done everything possible to make a happy life and a beautiful home for our family. They meant everything to me. Now it felt as if I was ripping all that to shreds. There was a huge sense of loss about leaving my home and putting an end to the family we used to be. I was looking back at something that was in the past. There would never be another family dinner around the table, or another Christmas, or a birthday. I wasn't just leaving a place, I was leaving a life and taking the certainty of our future as a family away from all of us. I was overcome with sadness at this thought.

'You must be very happy today,' Raymond said after I dropped Joe at school that morning.

'What do you mean?' I asked. By now, the moving van had arrived and the men were in and out with boxes. I was still packing clothes into suitcases.

'Well, you're moving away from us,' he said. 'It's what you wanted.'

'No, Raymond. I'm not happy. I couldn't be sadder.'

Maybe I had made the decision to leave in my mind, but physically, it was a wrench. I would miss living in the home I had helped create, I would miss my dog, my cats, Melinda – who had worked with me for twelve years – and every part of the life that I had known until now. But most of all, I felt terrible for my son.

By the end of the day, I'd moved my possessions into the two-bedroom flat on the 26th floor of the apartment block, not far from Aberdeen Marina. It was well-appointed, clean and I could see the Marina from one of the bedrooms, but it felt small after the expanse of the houseboat. I'd never lived in anything so tiny before. With space being an extravagant luxury in Hong Kong, a standard apartment was under 600 sq. feet. This one was less than 500 sq. feet. It certainly didn't feel like home yet but it was comfortable enough and I knew it would be perfectly adequate for my needs. Raymond, meanwhile, had helped me sort out the internet. We had two internet routers and phone lines for the houseboat and he said he would cancel one and I could reinstate it in the new apartment since there was no point paying for a third account. I didn't really understand the ins and outs of it all but later that day the technician came to my flat and set up the account for me.

That evening, as I was settling into my first night alone in the apartment, Raymond rang.

'We've got no internet,' he said.

'I don't understand,' I replied. 'The technician only moved the one you told him to take. I've got the internet here, connected to the account you instructed me to take.'

And I guess for Raymond, that was the moment he broke.

'WHAT KIND OF A PERSON ARE YOU?' he exploded. 'You've left your son here without any internet connection. Joe can't do his homework. Come on, Joe! You speak to your mum. Tell her. TELL HER!'

'I'm not going to get involved,' I heard Joe objecting in the background.

Until now, Raymond had been calm, helpful even, but perhaps everyone has a moment where the reality of a situation hits them hard. I had left him. After twenty-two years of marriage, I had left him.

'I only moved what you told me to move,' I said again. 'I literally did what you told me to. What do you want?'

But it was no good – he raged on at me, then slammed the phone down. I felt terrible, of course, knowing that Joe couldn't do his homework that night. But at the same time, I saw this for what it was – a powerful expression of Raymond's rage and helplessness. He had to let me go because he had no choice, but now he was punishing me for leaving. I felt sad for him at this moment. He was losing everything, too, only it wasn't his decision, it was mine. For the first time, I sensed that he was out of his depth. I don't think he had ever believed I would leave him. But how much longer could we keep lying to ourselves?

The next few weeks were perhaps the worst and loneliest time of my life. I couldn't imagine how my mother had done it. Being apart from Joe was really difficult. I got up every morning and drove to the houseboat to take Joe to school, as I had done when I lived at home, because I was determined he wouldn't be inconvenienced by my decision. Then, after school, I drove him to his rugby training and I made sure that when he was at home Melinda was there to look after him. During the day, I was busy studying or working at the school.

I spent every night alone in the flat, coming to terms with my new situation. Life was difficult but true to his word, Martin had been in touch and was showing care. He had gone to America on business for a couple of months. While it was true that I was starting to care for Martin, I was nowhere near being able to cope with a new relationship. I needed time on my own. Those nights, in that tiny flat, were some of the saddest I have ever experienced and I cried myself to sleep many times. It wasn't the same grief that I had after my father died, but there was a definite sense of loss, an ache in my heart for something that had been so important to me and was now gone forever.

Then, in April, Raymond rang.

'When are you coming home?' he asked cautiously. The question took me by surprise but my feelings were clear. Now that I had made the difficult decision to leave, I couldn't go back.

'I... I don't think I am, Raymond. I'm not going to come home.'

'Well, I think it's the wrong decision.' I heard the crack in his voice.

'I'm not coming back, and I guess it's the decision I have to live with.' I felt he heard the resigned tone in my voice.

THE WATER RABBIT

Over the last few months, Raymond and I had stayed in touch, meeting up occasionally for dinner. We talked around things, we didn't really say much about the situation. What was there to say? He asked me to attend couples counselling, but for me, the time for talking was over. It seemed horribly ironic that it was now *him* asking *me* to go to therapy together. There were many times in the past I'd asked Raymond to go for counselling with me. I had asked him to re-evaluate our lives, to try and reconnect to save our marriage.

'Why would we do that?' he would say, or: 'I'm busy, I haven't got time for this.'

Well, now there was nothing left to talk about. I'd done my therapy. I'd nearly died. And now, I wanted *more*.

Occasionally, during these brief meetings, when I sensed Raymond was reverting to his awkward, difficult side, I'd sit back, relieved at the thought that I didn't have to go home with him. It was a good feeling. *I can walk away tonight. I don't have to be part of this.* Leaving home had been the hardest day of my life, but I knew I couldn't face doing it again. This had to be it. Raymond was silent for a moment, then he said: 'If you're not coming home, I'm not going to tolerate being married to someone who isn't going to live with me, so we may as well start the paperwork.'

'Yes,' I agreed. 'We might as well.'

And that was the start of our divorce.

It was a difficult time. Of all the years I have lived through, this was probably the hardest. Despite the many years of loneliness with Raymond, I'd never felt as alone as I did now. But there was also a sense of liberation and, now that I had found the courage to step outside of my life, I could look at it with different eyes. I hadn't realised until now how bad things had become and I felt huge relief that I didn't have to work hard anymore to keep the peace. All the tiptoeing around Raymond, the second-guessing and trying so hard to please him was over. For years I had dreaded going out to dinner together as a family. I didn't even realise how much I hated it until it stopped. Raymond would often criticise the children for not holding their chopsticks correctly or for saying something he disagreed with. It was the Chinese way and to Raymond, an expression of his parental love: *It's my job to make sure you know what you're doing. If I let that go I've failed you because someone is going to say – what kind of parent have you got that you don't know how to hold your chopsticks properly?*

However, as much as I understood where Raymond's behaviour differed from mine culturally, his habit of criticising had become the dominant force during our family time together. We could be having a discussion and one of the kids would say something about something they had read. And this would spark a reaction.

'That's a stupid way of thinking!'

'Well, I'm not saying I agree with it, Dad.'

'Well, why are you reading those kinds of rubbish books?'

It got to the stage where I didn't want to say anything because I couldn't be sure if it would trigger a family argument. The kids were entitled to an opinion and I appreciated that they wanted to discuss things. Wasn't sharing ideas a good way to learn and connect? I found our life uncomfortable and was constantly on edge, trying to keep the peace and swerve conflict. Leaving had given me the perspective to realise that I didn't want to do that anymore. In fact, it occurred to me that I had already tolerated the situation for far too long.

There were other things I knew I wouldn't miss. Raymond used to call me 'stupid' a lot. I didn't like it, but during our marriage I couldn't stop him and the insult became habitual.

'Don't be so stupid!'

THE WATER RABBIT

'Why are you stupid?'
'That's a stupid thing to say.'

It was a hurtful comment which dented my confidence over the years. After all, Raymond was the one with two degrees, I was the housewife who had never been to university and I felt intellectually inferior. Calling me 'stupid' all the time was like rubbing my nose in it. Well, that was changing. I was doing well at university, acing all my exams, excelling in class. I clearly wasn't stupid and during one argument before I left, I threw it back at him.

'Raymond, if I'm so stupid, how stupid does that make you, wanting to keep me?"

'Who are you talking about?' he yelled.

'Well, you must be stupid for staying with someone as stupid as me!'

Raymond had his own demons. By the end of our marriage I believe he was trapped in a corporate world which gave him no satisfaction or happiness. He had spent a lifetime trying to prove something to himself and to his mother who didn't want anything to do with him. When his father died two years earlier, we'd flown over to Ipswich for the funeral and Hannah came down on the train from Durham to meet us. She read a poem during the service. Afterwards, one of Raymond's uncles insisted we pay our respects to the family in the traditional way. It was expected of us. I was reluctant to make any direct contact and assumed that our presence was enough. Over the years, Raymond's mother had shown no indication of wanting anything to do with us or our children and I didn't want to expose the kids to any unpleasantness. But we were assured it would be okay. So we went into her home and, with a nod of encouragement from his mum's older brother, we lined up with the rest of the mourners to pay our respects to the bereaved. When we got to the front of the line, I introduced myself and the kids to Raymond's mother, a tiny woman with a stern face. It was the first time either of us had set eyes on one another, a strange moment after so many years of rejection. But as the children started to greet her, she interjected in a sharp tone: 'You are nothing to me. I have two other grandchildren who are better than you.' The kids just stood there, wondering what to do next that.

I was horrified at this outburst. How dare she speak to my children like that! I grabbed all three kids and told Raymond: 'We'll wait outside.'

He followed us out briefly to try to persuade us to go back in but I'd had enough.

'She's your mother. You do what you feel is best, but I'm not going back in there with the kids.'

Perhaps Raymond felt we needed to do this together, to face his mother once and for all. But I wasn't interested. I'd done what was requested, against my better instinct, and it had played out exactly the way I expected. We had made a special effort to all fly out to England for the funeral, only to be treated like dirt by Raymond's mother. It stung. And what made it all worse was the recollection of my father's funeral when Raymond hadn't even bothered to show up.

Raymond and I had each brought our own demons to the marriage. We were both poorly served by our mothers — for different reasons – but it seemed to me as if Raymond was never prepared to face his past. For me, counselling had helped me to recognise the damage I carried from my childhood. It meant I was a peace-maker, always opting to back down in order to avoid a scene. I didn't want history to repeat itself and I also didn't want to accept failure. But I had my needs too. I was in the prime of my life. I was well-read, vivacious, outgoing, constantly learning new things and, according to my friends, pretty decent company.

THE WATER RABBIT

And yet, within the marriage, I was always on my own.

But I was sick and tired of always being on my own and Martin had kept in touch. It was illness that finally brought us together once and for all. I had discovered a little patch of raised skin on the back of my thigh in early May and I must have caught it on something because it got infected and turned into cellulitis. At first, it was the size of a small coin but it grew to the size of a side plate and became burning hot. The doctor gave me antibiotics but it didn't get any better and when I went back a week later the infection was the size of a dinner plate and she insisted I go straight to hospital.

'But I can't,' I said. 'I've got to go to work tomorrow and I have an exam tomorrow night.'

Thankfully, she managed to get me seen by a specialist immediately who wanted to admit me straight away.

'It could become septicaemia if left untreated,' he warned. 'I can give you an injection of a different antibiotic and I'm going to draw a line round it but if it goes even 1 millimetre over that line in the next 24 hours you have to go straight to the hospital. I'll meet you there. Here's my emergency contact number.'

I went home that night and Reine came round to sit with me. I wasn't at all well and my temperature was all over the place. When the phone rang, Reine answered.

'Hi Raymond. I'm here with Carolyn because she's not well,' she told him. 'She's got a fever and the doctor said she might have to go to hospital.'

Aaron was back from university for summer break and he came round the next day.

'You look like you're going to die,' he said. 'I'm going to call Dad.' But when he spoke to his father, Raymond's response was clear.

'I'm not coming,' he said. So that was it. I was struck by a moment of clarity. The marriage, the relationship, it was gone and now I had to make the best of things on my own. Thankfully, with the support of friends and my son, I got through and managed to take my exams. The cellulitis started to regress and, after a couple of days, it shrank back down. I've still got a pockmark where it was originally. I realised that with divorce, there is a finality. You can't pick and choose the pieces of a marriage you want to keep or that are convenient to you. So when I got sick, I didn't have Raymond to rely on, he was not willing to help me. The relationship was over. I was well and truly alone.

Martin returned to Hong Kong in June and when he found out about the cellulitis, he was shocked and upset.

'You don't need to be on your own, Carolyn,' he said. 'I'm here for you. I want to be with you.'

And now, for the first time since he told me about his feelings, I was ready to be with him, too. The kids revealed Raymond also had a new woman in his life I realised that if he could move on, then I could too. I felt ready to explore my feelings for Martin and find out if we had a future together. Still, it felt awkward. Should I really be doing this? I felt guilty and judged by society. Was it okay for me to see someone else just a few months after leaving my husband? I didn't know what other people might think, so I was very careful about everything. I liked being with Martin, I liked how caring and attentive he was. And he really did seem to like spending time with me, which was wonderful. But I wasn't comfortable walking down the street holding hands or public displays of affection. Martin and I took a trip to Bali over the summer — our first holiday together as a couple - and that felt easier because I knew we wouldn't bump into anyone I knew there. It wasn't that I was ashamed to be with him. I was proud that he liked me, but I was nervous about committing to the relationship. I didn't want to screw this one up too.

THE WATER RABBIT

Gradually, Martin spent more and more time in my flat, but when Hannah came to visit during the summer, I sent him away for the day.

'Where's Martin?' Hannah asked when she arrived.

'He's not here. I want to spend time with you.'

'Hmmm... well, does he live here?'

"He does stay over, yes, but he's only got a backpack here.'

'Hmmm...'

She didn't say much but her disapproval was clear. By now, Hannah had graduated from Durham and it was a source of great sadness that I didn't go to her graduation. But at that point everything was still very awkward between me and Raymond and although I had a ticket to attend, I just felt it would be too difficult. Raymond and Joe went to see Hannah's ceremony and I watched a recording of it. I was so proud of her.

'Look, Hannah,' I said afterwards. 'It's important that my relationship with you is good. You mean everything to me. I know you don't like this but my relationship with your Dad is over. We are both entitled to move on and I know it doesn't feel good right now but I hope we can both be okay soon.' Hannah had a contemplative look, she was beginning to see as time went on that I had been unhappy for some time.

Martin moved in with me properly after the summer and we took time to adjust to living together. Keen to talk at the end of each day, we made a point of having 'catch up' time, sitting down with a cup of tea and sharing what each of us had been through. It felt so good to talk out loud about my experiences, for Martin to show an interest in what I was up to and to ask my thoughts and opinions about his life and plans. I felt heard! We got to know each other well during this time, understanding what upset, irritated or delighted the other, getting to know what made us both tick. By Christmas, all three children were home for the holidays but were due to spend Christmas Day with their dad. So I invited them over for drinks on Christmas Eve.

'Should I make myself scarce?' Martin offered as the evening approached. I thought about this for a second, but then I realised that it was time the kids understood that Martin was now an important part of my life.

'No,' I said. 'It's enough already. I want you here.'

They came over and actually it was really lovely. Aside from getting used to us as a couple, the kids all liked and got on with Martin, and it certainly felt as if tensions with Hannah were easing. I missed her and I suspect she missed me too. A couple of days after Christmas, she called to ask what I was doing for New Year's Eve. I'd never really been a fan of New Year's Eve but this year Martin and I had tickets to a black-tie event at the golf club in Deep Water Bay. Martin said we owed it to ourselves to see in the New Year in style.

'Well, I'll come over and do your hair for the evening,' she offered. So on 31 December she came over to my flat, curled my hair and did my make up. Once she finished, I looked great and I felt very grateful for her help. She looked at me in the mirror.

'Happy Birthday, Mum,' she smiled. She was right, exactly one year ago, I was near death, fighting for my life in the South China Sea. While my birthday is in fact earlier in December, in that moment, Hannah saw December 31st as new beginning. That was the moment I knew Hannah accepted my new life and my new partner.

'Thank you, Hannah,'

From this moment onwards everything felt right again between me and my daughter. It was such a relief. We had a turned a corner. In that moment I knew everything was going to be smooth sailing. We had both been through a difficult time but it meant the world to me to have her love and presence in my life.

THE WATER RABBIT

What an upheaval for us all, I thought, relieved as we hugged goodbye that night. *Exactly twelve months ago I was lost at sea, struggling to keep my head above the waves, desperately fighting for my life. Now here I am, living in a tiny flat with Martin, going through divorce proceedings, fighting for my life again.*

It had been a very tough year, but I was still standing. Through all the mess, pain and chaos, we had all survived and though things were far from perfect, I felt I had got through the worst, laying the foundations for better times ahead.

18

THE WATER RABBIT

WHEN WE first moved to Hong Kong and Raymond and I were trying to settle into society, people commented on our relationship.

'You're married to a Chinese person?' they'd exclaim, surprised. 'It's usually the other way round, isn't it? Usually, it's the Western guy with the Asian wife.'

Frankly, I found these 'observations' rude but it was a popular thought, shared by many in the circles we moved in, and one I didn't really know how to respond to at the time.

'Well, yes, I suppose we are unusual...' I'd shrug. That idea, of being *unusual*, of being different from everyone else was one that persisted throughout my life.

As a very young child growing up in a dysfunctional household, you have no idea how bad things are at first. There are no yardsticks, nothing to measure your life against, so you assume everything in your world is normal. It is only as you get older and glimpse into other people's lives that you realise yours is different. Mental illness was taboo when I was growing up – nobody talked about it, or if they did it was in hushed whispers, something to be ashamed of, something to sweep under the carpet. So when my friend's parents asked which hospital my mother was in, I wouldn't tell them it was Winwick, the mental hospital. I said I couldn't remember. It was an instinctive reaction, an idea that if they knew my mother was being treated for mental ill health that would put us on the outside. Then we would be judged and regarded as *other*.

And when a friend from high school came round to my house for the first time and asked why my parents slept in separate beds, I made up a fib and told her it was because my dad snored. It was a silly lie and easily contradicted, of course. My mother would still have heard my father snoring if they were in the same room. But it was her reaction that made me realise that their sleeping arrangements weren't normal. The way her nose wrinkled at the end, the quizzical look on her face. After that, I stopped inviting friends back to my house. What else wasn't normal? I wasn't keen on finding out, and after my mother left I certainly didn't want to invite others to view our peeling wallpaper and chipped plaster. Even if they were friends, there was a judgement in the way people noticed things. I didn't want them noticing any more ways in which we were different.

I had very little confidence growing up. It was hard when my own mother kept trying to leave or attempted suicide. Somewhere along the line I started thinking I wasn't worth staying around for. And when friends made comments or questioned the way we lived I withdrew further into myself. Context was key to this feeling. We lived in a nice, middle class area where everybody was doing well; homes were well-kept, marriages were stable. Contextually, we were odd. We had no money, no mother and we took our holidays in a field in North Wales. I was out of place, anomalous. We all look around for benchmarks and when we don't sit comfortably in our setting, it jars. I think that's where Raymond was, too. He'd given up his family to be with me, he had something to prove to himself and the family, to people who were racist to him when he was in the UK. The determination to make something of himself got a hold of him and became all-consuming.

But for all our differences as individuals, Raymond and I had created a strong unit. Together, we fitted each other and moved through life fairly well. Our partnership gave us both the confidence and reassurance to be *unusual*, to embrace our differences. Being the unusual couple in Hong Kong was a mantle I came to accept. And when I sat down at those black-tie dinners with the swanky banker set, I knew that my Lancastrian roots and down-to-earth conversation stood out amongst all the superficial nonsense. There were a lot of people out there trying to impress, showing off about their big cars and big houses, and these folk lacked a bit of good old-fashioned, tell-it-like-it-is *craic*. I may have changed my context but my personality never changed. I was the same old Carolyn whether I was at home with the kids, working at school in my job or swishing around fancy black tie events. I was interested in people, happy to tell a good joke and have a laugh. People were drawn to me because I didn't lord it over anyone, I was never impressed by material wealth and I valued honesty and good company. Hong Kong is a very glossy, materialistic place but I always went deeper with the people I befriended and it was this *ordinariness*, strangely enough, that made me stand out in Hong Kong. So there it was – I was always anomalous. And whereas it was uncomfortable to be *different* as a child and teenager, as an adult I got used to it. And even, I suppose, embraced it.

That was one reason it took so long for me to let our relationship go. Raymond and I found strength and confidence through our partnership. The whole was always greater than the sum of its parts. So dismantling the world we had created was a frightening prospect. Was I happy to be the misfit alone? Could my personality withstand this isolation in the world? In 2005, when I was becoming clinically depressed, I struggled with this

THE WATER RABBIT

sense of identity and belonging. I had spent many years being one half of the Carolyn/Raymond partnership, making our family and creating a happy home life but at the point where our children were becoming independent and living their own lives, I realised that my own was no longer fulfilling. I was searching for my identity. That was when I got the tattoo.

It was something I'd never really thought of before – after all, I had inherited a bourgeois distaste for tattoos from a time when they were associated with the 'lower classes'. But in the intervening years, the tattooing revolution had taken place. They were now mainstream and an acceptable form of body art. One evening, Raymond and I were having dinner with Raymond's colleague and his wife and conversation moved onto the subject of tattoos. The general mindset was that they were probably unseemly for our age group but at this moment I knew that I wanted one.

'Really?' Surprise rippled round the table. Perhaps it appeared out of character but then I had never really conformed to other people's expectations.

'Yeah, sure. Why not?' I replied. 'The only thing is it would have to be completely unique to me. I couldn't have an off-the-shelf design.'

Not long after this dinner I decided to follow through with my expressed desire. When my cousin Gareth – my mother's brother's son — had visited from the UK he had researched a famous tattoo artist to get a large dragon tattoo whilst he was staying with us. It took nine hours straight but I was very impressed with the results. This artist specialized in Japanese artwork, so I made an appointment to see her. I told her that in the Chinese Zodiac I was a Water Rabbit and since I identified strongly with the personality traits of this Zodiac animal, I asked her to draw me a design. She came up with a picture of the rabbit inside a wave. It was a really sweet design so I went ahead and had it tattooed on my right butt cheek. Aaron came with me. He said it looked awesome and told me I was cool. It felt good to have something that was truly unique to me. That was in 2005, two years before the accident. The extraordinary thing was that this image was an almost perfect representation of what happened to me. There I was, a rabbit in the sea, encased in waves.

It was beyond strange that I actually had a picture of this life-changing moment tattooed on my body two years before the event itself. But besides the correlation with the accident, I identified very strongly with the personality traits of the Water Rabbit. In feng shui, there are twelve Zodiac animals and five elements which can change the personality type of your Zodiac animal. For instance, Hannah is a Fire Rabbit and differs from me in crucial ways. Water Rabbits are noted as quiet but intellectual, polite and peaceful individuals. Though careful in life, we are highly regarded by others and dislike arguments and disputes. So we are thought of as lucky animals, peacemakers. We are slow to anger and prefer instead to turn a blind eye to something unpleasant in an effort to keep the peace. We are considered to be efficient workers with a good memory, perceptive and good at planning. Most notably, we are creatures who enjoy decorating and keeping a nice, clean home. This describes me almost down to a tee! I had always enjoyed making a beautiful home and in fact we had moved onto the houseboat Raymond designed in April 2005. A five-bedroom house over three storeys, it was the most amazing house I'd ever lived in and I spent many months choosing the décor and making it perfect.

Even today, my mind is always on improving my environment. What can I do to make a place look nicer or feel better? I put it down to the fact that I spent so long wishing for a nice home as a child, wishing my house was tidier, cleaner, more organised. It was never a question of extravagance, just of maintaining a pleasing, calming environment. I wanted things to be *nice*. From the moment we were first married, our cupboards were organised, the stairs hoovered and everything free of dust. We had a tiny little front and back garden but I never failed to mow the lawn or weed the drive. It was the same every time we moved — I kept our home in really good order. The irony is that the worst match for a Water Rabbit is a Rooster. And Raymond , of course, is a rooster.

I got my second tattoo in November 2007, a month before our disastrous sailing trip: the Red Rose of Lancaster sits on my left hip. It's the same rose on England rugby shirts and though I had spent just my earliest years there as a child, I wanted it because I was born in Lancashire and that was where my roots lay. My Grandad had said many times: 'Never forget where you came from'. And I felt that even though I had left England behind many years before, my personality and history were shaped by my past. My grandparents, in particular, had had a great influence on me. Though both had passed away many years earlier, I'd loved them enormously. Grandad had been a keen golfer, taught himself German and painted beautiful water colours. He had been a positive force in my early years, sticking up for me and Andrew many times when we were children, telling my father that Andrew would be okay after he dropped out of school because he was good with his hands. And he was right! Andrew runs a successful log stove fitting business now. He also assured my father I would be fine when I fell for Raymond: 'After all, you can't help who you fall in love with.'

Grandad was very down-to-earth about so many things and told us stories about his deprived childhood and how he was sent down the mines to earn his keep at fourteen. But he didn't like being underground and joined the RAF. Not long after that,

World War II broke out and he distinguished himself in his many missions flying Lancaster bombers with the RAF. I admired Grandad – he had changed his own destiny, rejecting the dark, subterranean mines to become a war hero in the skies. And yet he never changed who he was — honest, hardworking and proud of being a Geordie. It was his stories of flying during the war that entranced and inspired Aaron who trained to become a pilot not long after leaving university. To this day, he still flies with Grandad's RAF pin in his pocket. Sadly, Grandad got dementia and I went to see him in the home shortly before his death. When I left that day, I knew for certain I would not see him again and started to get very upset. He saw this and tried to reassure me: 'Don't worry, Bonny Lass, everything in the garden is rosy.'

Grandma died from a heart attack five months to the day after she lost him. Over the years their relationship with my mother had been up and down, but at the very end, she did something which I found unforgivable. She told Grandma she wanted to have Grandad's precious war medals framed and when Grandma finally agreed, Mum picked them up from Wales and promptly sold them to a collector in Milton Keynes. It was the final act of betrayal on the back of a lifetime of selfish indifference to others.

To me, the Red Rose of Lancaster was an important symbol of my past, a connection to those who had come before me. The rose, the rabbit — these were my stamps of identity. The rose signified the start of my life and the water rabbit was who I was now. Perhaps I needed those imprints on my body to remind me that I didn't need another person to validate me or my choices. I had the strength to face life on my own.

It was Raymond who started divorce proceedings in April 2008. In Hong Kong, divorcing couples are required to live apart for two years before officially applying for a decree absolute and during that time they are expected to sort out all financial arrangements so that, at the point of the final decree, the divorce itself is just a formality. We opted for a no-fault divorce. Though Raymond thought Martin was the reason for the breakdown in our marriage, I don't think it would have sat well with him to lay the blame officially for our break-up at another man's door. We both accepted the marriage was over and it had nothing to do with anyone else. There was a lot to sort out: several different properties, bank accounts as well as cars, a wakeboard boat and the insurance pay-out from the yacht. It took quite a bit of time and a fair amount of back and forth but in the settlement we came to, I was given a lump sum and the small house in Peterborough we had bought so the kids could live near my sister whilst they were on leave from university. Raymond stayed in the houseboat and agreed that I could live in the Hong Kong apartment we owned as long as I wanted. It was a very comfortable four-bedroom apartment with a roof garden and since we'd never lived in it as a family, I was more than happy to move in with Martin. There was enough space for the kids to stay over too. Raymond stipulated that when it was sold, I would take a fixed sum. There was only one condition on this arrangement. If I wanted to remarry, I either had to sell the apartment or buy out Raymond's half. I understood his reasoning for this and felt it was quite fair: after all, he didn't want to retain a connection to my finances if I was married to someone else.

According to my lawyer, I could have negotiated a larger settlement, but I had reached the stage where I was more interested in preserving a good relationship for the sake of the kids than a prolonged fight. We agreed that the children needed to be financed through university and Raymond took on that responsibility. I was just one person after all, I didn't need anything more than he was offering, and I had come to resent the constant obsession with money. I had seen how Mum's greed had taken everything from Dad. How we had to struggle through high school. How much money does one person really need? Besides, I didn't want to live off my ex-husband for the rest of my life. I was determined to forge a path in Hong Kong on my own, with or without a man, and had decided to develop myself professionally so I could earn my own money. This was a familiar feeling to the one I'd had when I left school. I wanted independence, to make my own choices and keep some perspective on what I really needed. Balance was important to me. I was only too aware of how an extreme lifestyle came at a cost. So we came to an acceptable financial agreement and the children would be looked after.

The divorce was finalised in March 2010 and three months later I graduated from my course with a first class honours degree in Criminology. I found it faintly ironic that Raymond, who had never been convinced of the value of my university career, was no longer around to find out that I had done exactly as he'd asked: I passed the course with flying colours. Martin, however, was thrilled.

'I couldn't be prouder of you,' he said at my graduation.

How funny my life was turning out to be, I marvelled. Here I was with the most wonderful, caring, supportive and loving life partner I could imagine and I'd met him in a bar in Wanchai, a notorious late-night drinking spot! Anyone who washed up in Wanchai was only ever one drink away from oblivion. The worst possible advice I could imagine giving another human being was to go down Wanchai to pick a future partner. And yet that is exactly what I'd done. But then, when had I ever done the *usual* thing?

19

BY YOUR SIDE

IN TIME, Martin moved to Hong Kong permanently and set up his own security company, while I went on to do a Master's in Counselling. Raymond kept his promise to finance the children through university so they could start their lives debt-free, and I was proud that they all applied themselves well to their studies, making good choices, developing their careers and finding wonderful life partners. Raymond moved on too, re-marrying not long after the divorce. Martin's ex also remarried.

'What about us?' Martin asked frequently. 'Will you marry me?'

'Why?' I'd say. 'There's no point. Besides, if we get married we'll have to move out of the apartment. Would it really make any difference to our lives? We're happy. Let's just leave it at that.'

It was true. I was blissfully happy with Martin in a way I'd never imagined possible. He was caring and supportive and always told me he loved me. He wouldn't leave the house or put the phone down without saying it! It was harder for me – I wasn't used to making public declarations of my affection and struggled to say 'I love you' back but that didn't mean I didn't feel it. We enjoyed an equal partnership, one where decisions were made jointly and household chores were not automatically assigned to me. If I was busy with my studies, Martin would offer to make dinner and if the kids needed us for anything, we were both there to help. Martin established a trusting, supportive relationship with all the kids, very much treating them as if they were his own while I also developed a close relationship with his daughter, Ysobelle. As for me, I felt cared for and valued in a way I hadn't in a very long time. Martin could tell what I was feeling just from the look on my face and always asked and wanted to know what was wrong. He noticed if I wasn't happy and he worried about my welfare. But whenever he asked me to marry him, I refused. I just couldn't do it. I didn't trust myself not to screw it up again. While I loved being with Martin I didn't feel the need to go traipsing up the aisle again. Until that is, I got a special message.

We had flown over to the UK for a holiday when we decided to take a trip up to Yorkshire to visit my dear friends, Marian and Derek. Marian had not met Martin before and, seeing as we were so close, I thought it was high time I introduced them. When we got up to their house in Richmond, Marian and Derek were thrilled to see us both and while Martin and Derek went off to play golf for the day Marian said she had a little surprise in store.

'I've got an appointment for us to see a psychic!' she confided. 'I need to know when I'm going to be a Grandma — if ever — and I think you should have a reading too.'

'What for?'

At this stage of my life, I really didn't think I was searching for anything in particular. But perhaps we are none of us immune to the desire to know the future and my curiosity was piqued.

We got in my hire car for the half-hour drive to Darlington. On the way, I caught Marian up with all the news from our friends out in Hong Kong.

'You know, Carolyn, it's funny but me and Derek are the only couple that stayed together from all the people we knew from those days,' Marian reflected. 'All the other couples split up and went on to second partnerships. And they've all been a lot better for it — really successful. Just look at you! Martin is amazing. He's such a nice guy.'

'Yeah, he is,' I smiled. I thought Martin was great, of course, but it was always nice to hear that my friends approved of him too.

'So, will you marry him?' she asked.

'No, I'll not marry Martin.'

'Why not?'

'Well, what's the point?'

'Ah, come on...'

'No. I'll not marry Martin, Marian, so stop going on about it.'

Once we arrived at the psychic's house, we waited in the hallway before he came out and introduced himself as Hughie, then he took each of us one by one into another room for our reading. I went in first. Hughie fixed me with a serious look and said: 'Now then, Carolyn, why won't you marry that man?'

I was taken aback. I hadn't said a word at this point. I certainly hadn't told him anything about my life.

'What do you mean?' I asked guardedly. Though I had visited a couple of psychics in the past, that didn't mean I was gullible. My attitude was: tell them nothing, see what they can tell you.

'I know, Carolyn, that even on the drive here you've been saying that you won't marry him. And it's probably because you're worried about *fucking it up* but you won't be able to *fuck it up* because he loves you more than you will ever know. And he tells you that every day and you don't tell him back.'

Jesus! I couldn't believe it. I couldn't believe it. I actually interrogated Marian later to make sure she hadn't shared any details about me. She swore blind she hadn't. How could he know these things? I sat there, keeping as blank an expression as possible, as he went on: 'You were married before but you weren't treated as well as you should have been and you shouldn't let anybody push you around. You've got three children, but they're getting older now whereas the man you're with – who is really good-looking by the way — has got a daughter, much younger.'

Oh my god, this is all true. Still, I didn't speak.

He added: 'You don't have anything to do with your mother but you didn't need her before so you don't need her now.'

'Well,' I said slowly. 'I have to say you're correct so far...'

All of a sudden the room went cold and little goosebumps rose up along my arms.

'Do you feel cold?' he asked.

'Yeah, I do.'

'Well, look at my arm. I'm freezing. All the hairs are standing on end.'

'Yeah, it's really cold,' I agreed as a chill ran up my spine.

'That's because your Dad has arrived. Your Dad's got a message for you....'

Dad? Suddenly my heart was in my mouth. I hadn't said anything to this man about my father. He didn't even know Dad was dead.

'Your Dad says he's sorry he's not around to meet the man you're with now because he thinks he would like him very much. And if you want to get married again he will still be standing next to you.'

I started to cry. *Is he really here? Is that possible?* I didn't know what to think. All I knew was that this psychic was 100 percent right about every part of my life, and now he had brought a message from my father. Would it really be okay for me to marry again?

Later, I mulled this thought over in my mind. Perhaps, deep down the real reason I didn't want to get married again was because I felt ashamed that my marriage to Raymond had ended. All this time I carried a sense of shame that I had failed somehow. Maybe it was time to let that go.

Martin and I travelled a lot together. We went to Cornwall during the summers. It was great to have my travel buddy with me. Cornwall, was where Martin's parents Betty and Arthur lived. Arthur was a kind and gentle person. He would do anything to help anyone, never grumpy and always charming. A retired carpenter and builder, he busied himself with helping folk out with little odd jobs. If a neighbour needed their door rehanging or a shelf fixing, Arthur would potter over and get it done. He had high standards and frequently said that if you are going to bother doing a job, make sure you do it well. Betty was more robust, she came across as slightly bossy in a no-nonsense, say-it-like-it-is kind of way. The first time she met me at their cottage she reached out and hugged me. I felt a bit awkward at first, unused to such an effusive welcome. But she seemed to take to me immediately. Betty was a talker, always telling a story or relaying an episode from the past. She could talk for ages and I learned a lot about Martin from her. She knitted and was very involved in village life. Having lived in St Just since 1969, Betty and Arthur were a well-known and much liked couple with many friends. They both seemed to be content with their lot and did a lot of community activities, such as fundraising for charity and supporting the local cricket club. It's fair to say I liked them both enormously.

They came to visit us in Hong Kong and Betty would sit in the evening, clacking her knitting needles while we chatted.

'You know, Betty,' I said once. 'Martin tells me he's never been happier than he is with me.'

She looked me in the eye: 'And he's telling the truth. I know my son.'

'Yes, but he's always worrying about you both, getting older...'

'I don't know why he worries about us,' she tutted. 'We're alright. We've lived our life, you just need to get on with yours.'

Martin's daughter Ysobelle would come down for a week or two every summer to stay with her grandparents and that's when Martin could spend precious time with her, too. St Just is an old mining town, the most westerly town in the UK, six miles from Land's End. I was knocked out when I first visited. It was so peaceful. I woke the first morning to the sound of the cows in the field. The air was fresh with a hint of salt. The scenery was spectacular, a coastline peppered with prehistoric relics, mine ruins, standing stones, and wonderful sandy beaches. There didn't seem much point in owning a property in Peterborough anymore, so I sold the house and Martin and I decided to invest in a place in Cornwall. But after two years, we just couldn't seem to find a suitable property. We viewed a lot of 'barns for renovation' but nothing seemed right. Still, I followed the property websites and one day noticed that Martin's old family home was up for sale and had been for some time.

'That's your old place, isn't it?' I said.

'Yes, but it's a seven-bedroom property,' he said. 'We don't want that.'

'Well, it doesn't say seven bedrooms on the estate agent details. They must have rejigged some of the rooms or put in extra bathrooms.'

Martin came over to look at the details online. We flicked through the pictures of his childhood home, a house which his parents had run as a B&B for thirty-two years before retiring. Since then it had been through two more owners but it looked like it was now in need of some serious TLC.

'Oh, look! It's all overgrown,' Martin frowned. 'It's a bit of a mess. It wasn't like that when Mum and Dad had it.'

'No? Well, I'd like to look at it when we go back to Cornwall.'

I couldn't explain it, but I had a good feeling about this house.

In August 2013, during our annual visit to Cornwall, we made an appointment to view the 200 year old mine captain's house. It was just three doors down from Martin's parent's cottage so we could walk there from their home. And as soon as I stepped over the doorstep, I knew I could live there.

'I love it! I love it so much,' I breathed. The old granite house was full of character and warmth. Martin too was struck by an immediate sense of belonging, after all he had grown up in this house.

'It feels different from when I lived here,' he said. 'It's familiar but also changed.'

We had a good look around and though it needed a lot of work, I could see huge potential.

Returning to Martin's parents' cottage that afternoon, we met Arthur in the front garden.

'So what do you think of the house?' he asked.

'I love it!' I said. 'It needs a bit of work but it could be the answer to what we want. It's got spare bedrooms, a couple of bathrooms. It's really nice.'

Just then, I noticed a sparrow hawk sitting on the fence post. I recognised the bird of prey straight away because the sparrow hawk is on Dad's coat of arms.

'Blimey, a sparrow hawk!' Arthur exclaimed. 'You don't normally see them, they're a bit secretive.'

'Mmmm... isn't it beautiful?' I smiled.

The sparrowhawk fixed its gimlet eyes on me. Then it took off and soared right over the old family home, circling it, spreading its expansive wings over the rooftop before flying off into the distance.

'I think we'll get it,' I said decisively. 'I think it'll be the best thing we ever did.'

We spent the next three years carrying out an extensive renovation which involved a full rewiring of the house, fitting a new boiler, new windows, a complete overhaul of the garden, new bathrooms, radiators and a renovation of the self-contained extension. It wasn't easy arranging it all from afar but Arthur helped a lot, sourcing materials and labour as well as overseeing the work. He was well-respected and knew all the trades folk from his working days. Now the house seemed to give him a new lease of life. He wandered over most days, keeping an eye on the renovations, even carrying out some of the ground-level work himself. He was thrilled with how it was coming along and was happy the house was being brought back to life, though with Martin's money, not his own! It really was our passion project and well worth it in the end because the finished house is beautiful. Our Cornish home has given us all a place to be together in the UK. It's our home away from home and whenever we are in the UK to see Martin's daughter or if any of our kids are over there, we tend to get together there.

'It's more than just a home,' Hannah said to me. 'It's a gathering place.'

And I think she's right — the house brings us all together. It's got a strange feel to it that it needs people in it and when we're all there it looks after you. The kids certainly appreciate having a base in the UK, which is after all where their mother came from and where we still retain strong connections. For Martin, it's like coming full circle. He grew up there, left to join the army, went all over the world but he's come back to the very house he left at nineteen.

The final piece of the puzzle came together in late 2017, when Raymond and I decided to sell the apartment. The housing market was buoyant and we were both keen to remove that final attachment to one another. Hannah had recently married and moved back to Hong Kong with her husband Angelo. They were over for a visit when I told them that it looked like the sale of the apartment was going through.

She smiled.

'That's great news, Mum. So I guess you and Martin can get married now.'

It was true – the last obstacle had been removed.

'Do you think we should?' I asked.

'Everybody's been going on about it for all these years so yes, I think you should!' she laughed. Martin and I looked at one another, the question lingering in the air between us. I knew how happy it would make him if I finally agreed to a wedding, and I no longer felt any shame in the idea of getting married again. Besides, in the past few years we had watched his parents struggling in their old age. Arthur was in poor health and Betty needed care for dementia. They had been together so many years and I could see that being married had been vital in allowing them to access the right care. Next of kin, probate, these issues mattered when half of a couple became incapacitated. Time was marching on for all of us. It seemed to me a sensible, practical move.

'Well, we could go down to City Hall and sign the papers,' I suggested.

Martin sighed and rolled his eyes.

'For goodness sake, you're not doing that, Mother!' Hannah exclaimed in exasperation. 'That is ridiculous. You've got all these people who want to see you get married and you think you're going to City Hall with two strangers off the street? Forget it!'

'All right, all right,' I laughed. 'We'll do it properly then. We'll plan it for Cornwall.'

****

22nd July 2019, Cape Cornwall

Martin took my hand and looked me in the eyes, his voice quivering only slightly as he read the vows he had written for this moment.

'Love isn't perfect,' he said gently. 'It's not a fairy tale or a storybook, and it doesn't always come easy. Love is overcoming obstacles, facing challenges, fighting to be together, holding on and never letting go. I swear, Carolyn, I will do anything I can to make you happy. Now today, I am so happy to marry you and we can continue our journey.'

I felt a lump in my throat, but I had to keep it together because now was my turn. We had chosen to write our own wedding vows because, well, who knew better how to express the feelings we had for each other than us? For me, the words came so easily, it felt as if they had been waiting to be said for a long time.

'Martin, I promise to bring out the best in you because you bring out the best in me. Today, I am marrying my best friend. Thank you for always making me feel significant and for loving me unconditionally. I see these vows not as promises but as privileges: I get to laugh with you and cry with you, care for you and share my life with you.'

It was the most beautiful day I could imagine. We exchanged our vows in front of eighty of our closest family and friends gathered at the Cape Cornwall Club, overlooking the sunset and the ocean on the very edge of the Cornish coast. The weather was perfect, and we married at 5 p.m. so we could catch the sunset. The moment was exquisite, poetic. I couldn't believe that so many of my dearest friends flew all the way from Hong Kong and other far flung countries just to see us get married. But I suppose, after waiting such a long time, ours was a long-overdue invitation.

Perhaps because it had taken us so long to get here that it felt even more meaningful. Martin cried, his daughter cried, all my kids were tearful... there was barely a dry eye in the house by the time the celebrant declared us husband and wife. Then we had a great big Cornish party.

We had organised our wedding for the Monday after the town had held its own festival Lafrowda, so it felt like a wonderful continuation of the festivities. It all took a lot of work – once you start planning, these things take on a life of their own – but, my goodness, it was worth it in the end and I loved every single second. We had a pianist perform during dinner and my friend's son sang an aria before dessert. Then there was a fantastic band and later we partied with the help of a DJ until the early hours. The celebrations were only tinged with sadness by the fact that Arthur had recently passed away and Betty was now in a home. But we toasted them both at the table and I was just pleased they had been around long enough to see their old home brought back to life and Martin and I happy together. We had made a lasting commitment to each other in a stunning setting, a place that felt like home to us both. Our love may have been forged in the crucible of a crisis but over the years we had found lasting contentment and peace with each other, something neither of us ever took for granted.

20

THE MOTHERSHIP

Hong Kong, May 2021

I FOUND OUT about her death through a WhatsApp message. I had often wondered over the years how I would feel when my mother finally passed away. After all, I had not spoken to her since 1994 and, other than an odious letter she wrote not long after our move to Hong Kong, there was no real attempt on either side to mend the relationship, much to my sister's annoyance. The first Christmas I went back home after our move Elizabeth relayed to me how miserable her life had become since we left because Mum never stopped complaining about how we'd taken away her grandchildren.

'Can't you just make up with her?' she'd begged.

'Why? So that your life becomes easier? No, Elizabeth. You don't know what happened. You don't know what she did to me. I'll tell you if you like…'

But Elizabeth wasn't interested in hearing things from my point of view and I felt that my mother's attempts to manipulate others to do her bidding was just one more reason not to allow her back into my life.

Her letter, when it came, was a five-page diatribe, full of the usual accusations and insults. I was an evil daughter, I'd taken away her grandchildren, how dare I upset her like this. How dare I treat her like this. There was no attempt to reach out to me, no remorse, no understanding at all of how her own behaviour had led us to this point. She was completely blind to her own faults and, just as Grandma had said many years before, she was never going to change. I only read that letter once, then threw it away. Not once did she say she loved or missed me. Not once did she show any love, compassion or kindness. In my later years, especially after studying for my MA in Counselling, I started to read up on Narcissistic Personality Disorder and saw in that description an accurate portrait of my mother.

Over the years, I had felt grateful that she was out of my life, though this attitude often put me at odds with many people in Hong Kong, expats especially, who spoke fondly of the family they had left behind and how hard it was to be away from the parents they loved. I was gloriously free of that worry, though when I explained that I didn't speak to my mum because we were estranged, people would often project their own feelings onto the conversation.

'Oh, that's terrible! Are you not going to attempt to build any bridges?' they'd ask.

'No.'

'But she's your mother!'

'Well, that is precisely why I will not have anything to do with her. A mother should not, in my world, be as she was.'

I suppose most of us have a pretty good idea of how a mother should behave to their children, the traits and qualities that would allow them to maintain and nurture their relationship with their offspring. My mother was lacking in these, which wouldn't be so bad if she wasn't actually *my mother*. You could forgive – or at least forget – a distant aunt, for example, who was neglectful, abusive, selfish, cruel and exploitative. You could cut them out of your life very easily. But to be treated like that by the very person who, in your mind, was supposed to care for and be there for you, was totally unacceptable. You can't go back from it. I felt I had tried my best over the years and the way she behaved towards me was evidence that she couldn't change. If I had anything more to do with her it would only lead to more heartache, pain and trauma. As Grandma had said on many occasions she was like that 'from the day she was born' so to expect her to be any different was naïve.

My sister suggested I had made the mistake of getting too close to Mum and that our relationship had fallen apart because we had lived together in those weeks prior to our departure to Hong Kong.

'You should have kept your distance,' she insisted. But I can't believe our paths would have altered all that much if we hadn't moved in with her. There was always going to be a point at which our relationship would come to a head. Her actions, her behaviour, her thoughts and her words, everything pointed to an extreme form of selfishness throughout her life which, in the end, was too destructive for me to tolerate. Did I really have to put up with it just because she was my mother?

On the flipside of that, I thought about Raymond's mother and how she had disowned him when he began dating me. She didn't even want to meet me to decide whether she liked me or not. I found that very cold. Perhaps she thought at some point Raymond would relent and dump me. But as we got closer and more committed she dug her heels in, and then it was very hard for her to come back from her 'You're dead to me' comment. It was my dream to have kids who were bilingual and bicultural. But the only woman who could have helped that happen and taught them about the Chinese festivals was the one person who wouldn't have anything to do with them. Raymond's mother perhaps loved him too much, or at least her version of love, which equated to control, was too overpowering for her to allow him to grow into his own man. Mine didn't love me enough. Two sides of the same coin.

Mum had been in a home for five years at the time of her death. She had Alzheimer's and had stopped eating some months before. Gradually she retreated further and further inside herself until, at the end, she was little more than a tiny fragment of a woman. Thin, papery skin on fragile bones. No words. No sign of the powerful personality that had propelled her through life. My initial reaction on being told of her death was one of relief that her suffering was over. Alzheimer's is a terrible disease and I was glad that for her, it was now finished. The thing was, there was no more emotion after that. I kept expecting to experience something else but it never came. No sadness, no regret, no anger — nothing. I had long since let go of any resentment or remorse for the mother I never had. Her power to affect me had diminished with every year of our estrangement and now, in a perfect reflection of how she had behaved towards me as a child, I realised that she simply didn't matter to me anymore. She had gone a long time ago.

They organised the funeral within the Covid restrictions of the time. My sister wanted a simple cremation but Mum's husband Alan insisted on a service. Elizabeth fretted that there wouldn't be many people in attendance and that Mum's funeral – and therefore her life – would look small and inconsequential. But it wasn't too bad in the end. Along with Elizabeth, her husband Simon and their daughter, my brother attended with his sons. So between them all, they formed a party which made her funeral appear to be for a woman whose life was properly mourned. I read the order of service on WhatsApp and it seemed very appropriate, very tasteful. Just one reading and a couple of songs, including her favourite band Queen's mournful anthem,

Who wants to live forever? Perhaps in the end, Covid restrictions had made things a little easier. There weren't many people at *any* funerals during that period. And there was never a question that I would be there. Aside from Covid travel bans, I wasn't a hypocrite. We had parted ways many years before. My sister went through her papers recently and discovered that she hadn't even turned up to court for our custody hearing. She really didn't want us. Mum had never loved me enough and it took me many years without her to find my own love for myself.

In the end, I just felt sorry for her. She was unhappy, dissatisfied and restless most of her life. It wasn't a particularly joyful existence. Perhaps some small part of me mourned the loss of a mother I never had, but even then, I couldn't feel bitter about what might have been. In the end, she was my mother and though not pleasant at the time, I don't think it did me any lasting harm. I'm the person I am today *because* of her. It may sound like a cliché but we are all shaped by our past and I grew up wanting to be the absolute antithesis of her. My greatest pleasure today comes from my relationship with Martin, my children – including Martin's daughter – and my grandchildren. And it is both a source of pride and amusement that my nickname is now 'The Mothership'. One of the boys coined it because lots of friends come to me for care and advice, and it just stuck. I don't think that would have happened if I hadn't had her for a mother. For better or worse, she moulded me so how can I possibly hate her for that?

Today, every single moment spent with my family is precious, and perhaps I appreciate it all the more because of that fateful day at sea when I nearly lost my life. I am fortunate that Hannah and Angelo who work in finance, live in Hong Kong with their sons Leonardo and Raffaello. Aaron is a pilot and married to Chloe. They are also based in Hong Kong with their son Ewan.

THE WATER RABBIT

We see them all very regularly. Joe now lives in Denmark with his Danish girlfriend Sara, a lawyer, and works as an aerospace engineer. I am thrilled that my kids are with partners of a different nationality. Now my grandchildren will be bilingual and bicultural. Martin's daughter Ysobelle has just finished university in the UK and is now taking her first steps into the world.

Martin and I live a very quiet but content life. It's not the glamorous one I had with Raymond, but then we're nearing sixty and my idea of a good time has changed considerably as I've aged.

One thing I don't do any more is sail. I had no outright aversion to sailing after the accident. There were outings, races and regattas and I was happy to crew for Simon and Louise occasionally as I trusted them as a good sailors. But I didn't really like it. One time we were at the start of a race and the wind was up at 25 knots. The start of any race is always a precarious time because you've got everybody fighting for space and the boats get quite close. It's stressful in the best conditions but in high winds, it's a real nightmare. Simon asked us to tack and I was on the winch. He was in the middle of yelling some instruction when I could tell instantly something was wrong because the sails seemed to be getting looser instead of tightening up, which is what my winch was meant to be doing. I looked up and saw that the forestay – the metal wire that holds the mast up at the front to the bow of the yacht – had snapped and the whole mast was about to collapse. We immediately abandoned the race and got out of the way of the other yachts. We rapidly took the sails down to avoid the pressure pulling the mast down. I helped manoeuvre the yacht round to the boat yard, but the whole experience was a disaster. At least it was all over fairly quickly and we were not far from land, but at that moment I realised I didn't need this kind of stress in my life.

It was clear that my sailing days were behind me. As much as I wanted to move on and forget, my body retained the memory of everything I'd been through during the accident. That memory was jogged again during a day trip round Hong Kong in a junk. It's a fairly common leisure activity here to take junks out on day cruises round the islands where you anchor up and jump off the back of the boat and swim around with floats. But the first time I jumped off the back of a junk after the accident I got a shock. As soon as the saltwater hit my lips, I had an immediate flashback to being in the water during the disaster. I recalled sinking under the waves, swallowing masses of seawater and then rising up to the surface only to retch it all out again. My arms reached out instinctively for one of the floats in the water. I needed to grab hold of something solid. I needed to stay above the surface.

Over the years, it got to the point where even the motion of the waves, that feeling of moving up and down, was no longer pleasant. Before I left my job to embark on my new career, I accompanied a group of school children on a trip to Fiji and we had to cross between the islands on a catamaran. During one crossing, the sea was rough from a storm the night before and the catamaran kept lifting up and smashing back down on the starboard side. It was horrendous — everyone was either screaming or being sick. For twenty minutes, I was absolutely terrified. That motion of the swells brought it all back again — the slamming, the noise, the motion of rising up and smashing back down, exactly how it had been in *Purple X* during the storm. Afterwards, I had a blinding, adrenaline headache. There was no question — my body held memories of the trauma that I simply couldn't erase.

Thankfully, for the children it was different. None of them experienced the same trauma in the sea, so they weren't unduly affected. Hannah and Angelo owned their own boat for a while, Joe is a qualified sailing instructor and has taken a sailing holiday with mates round the Greek Islands and occasionally sails in Denmark, while Aaron enjoys wakeboarding. So the incident certainly didn't put my children off sailing for life.

Raymond and I now have a cordial relationship. We don't speak often, but we communicate if we need to for the sake of the children and grandchildren. I never saw Lars again after the disaster – he was, after all, one of Raymond's work colleagues. Paul still hung around the yacht club for a while afterwards, but when he moved back to Australia we lost touch. Victor returned to sailing and delivering yachts straight after the accident, and as far as I know he is still doing that. About a year after the accident, Joe saw someone walking past the porthole of the houseboat and he recognised the shoes. It was Victor who had come to pay us a visit. Sadly, I never got to see him because by then, I had moved out and I haven't seen him since. I do wonder sometimes how the accident affected them all and how often they think about what happened.

It was Sirpreet I wanted to find, and a few years after the accident I tracked him down. After leaving Maersk, he went to work in Dubai. Martin was over there for his own work and managed to look him up and visit him in his house. That first night, Martin said they sat up all night, reminiscing and crying. It was an emotional reunion for them both. Then Sirpreet came to Hong Kong on business in October 2012, and I met him at the White Stag in Wanchai of all places! It was so moving to see him again, to set eyes on the man who had saved my life, who had given me a second chance. How to even put into words what he meant to me? I couldn't begin.

And then in 2013, Martin and I spent Christmas in Dubai and we caught up with Sirpreet and his whole family there.

Meeting his family was wonderful. He has a lovely wife, three boys, one of whom is a pilot like Aaron, and I even got on well with his mother. One of the first officers from the Maersk was also living in Dubai at this time, so he and his wife came over and we had a little party. Sirpreet and I got on so well together and still message each other from time to time. I will always feel immense gratitude towards him and it has been so meaningful to be able to share that with him and his family through the years. But there's something more to it than that. For whatever reason, our lives our bound together by an invisible thread that I find both inexplicable and also impossible to ignore. He is the link between my old life and my new one.

The funny thing is Sirpreet and his crew never got any recognition from Maersk. Not a thank you, a phone call, a letter, nothing at all. The rescue was mentioned in dispatches at the board meeting but the crew itself never heard from Maersk themselves. When I was researching this book, I approached Maersk to see what records they kept of the rescue. They had nothing. Not a single document. They claimed not to have even heard of Sirpreet Kahlon, the master in command of their ship during a valiant and heroic rescue at sea. Perhaps this was to be expected – after all, more than ten years had passed since the disaster and records are not required to be kept beyond that time frame. But after fourteen years, I couldn't let this story be lost to the waves. There had to be some record, a written account of the heroism and seamanship of the men and women who saved the lives of seven complete strangers.

After all, who were we to them? We were nobody. They had no links to us, no obligations to rescue us. It's true that maritime law exists to compel you to act a certain way but there were other ships in the area and they didn't assist. There is the law and then then there is a higher morality that exists within us all. The brave crew of the *Maersk Princess* put their lives on the line to save us. It is hard to believe that people who you've never met would go to so much trouble to save your life and yet that is what happened. And though every single person on that ship played their part in the rescue, credit must go to Sirpreet who led the mission. His courage and skills were tested to the very limit on the night of 31 December 2007 and he rose to the occasion.

So, to the Captain and all the crew of the *Maersk Princess* of 31 December 2007, thank you.

On behalf of myself, my family and all those affected by your heroic actions, thank you all. Grandad flew Lancaster bombers in the RAF during the Battle of Britain and their motto resonates strongly with me. After all, in whatever way we choose to live our lives, I believe we can all aspire to raise ourselves up a little higher, to express in its fullest terms, our own humanity:

Per Ardua Ad Astra
Through Adversity to the Stars

Epilogue

Captain of My Ship

Leaving Hong Kong, 2022

I CAN ONLY be myself. I am many things to many people, fulfilling different roles. I needed to understand my true values and what I wanted my life to look like. It took me quite a long time to figure out who I was, what I valued and what I wanted. And every step on that journey was an opportunity to learn more. When people ask if I regret taking the trip to the Philippines, I say no. Nothing is a wasted opportunity. I would never have moved to the next phase of my life if it hadn't been for that ill-fated trip. All these experiences moulded me into the person I am today. I could never say.... 'It was a mistake to set sail from the Philippines.' Or 'I should never have married Raymond.' Or 'It was a mistake to cut Mum out of my life.' Some things may have been hard and painful at the time but were experiences where I grew the most. I wouldn't be *The Mothership* unless I had been through everything in my life to date. I have no regrets. I look at it all as part of the journey and every experience shaped me and my sensibilities.

I wouldn't swap my life for anyone else's. I make choices, keep going and steadily, life unfolds before me. My sister said to me a couple of years ago: 'You can say you've lived a full life, Carolyn, a very full life. Many people cannot say that, including myself.'

I think that is true. Some people never want to take risks. They may have grandiose plans of things they would like to do, but they are just fantasies if they don't take even the first step towards doing them. I wanted to know what was on the other side of the hill. I decided to start climbing. I was also stuck in situations, ready to live with a certain level of discontentment because of the fear of change. That sense of: 'I want to know but I don't want to go...' The impetus to change my circumstances depended on how much I wanted to see the other side of that hill. It could be fantastic or it could be terrible but was the not knowing more painful?

Maybe I held onto my marriage to Raymond longer than I should have done and certainly a fear of change was a factor that held me back. But there were other underlying reasons which were unique to me and my past. With my parents' relationship disintegrating so early, I didn't really know what a good marriage looked like so it was hard to judge if I was being unduly demanding. The only role models I had growing up were my grandparents who'd been together since the war. Back in those days, when a couple got married, the wife gave up her job and their role was then solely to be a 'wife'. To some extent this was the model I had tried, albeit subconsciously, to emulate. The only problem was that this didn't fit with modern life and it didn't fulfil me. Grandma instilled in me the belief that marriage was for life and not to give up when things got rough. She was very judgmental about Mum and it's true that Mum was selfish, but she was also unhappy. Grandma held the belief that divorce was the easy way out. So I struggled on.

As a capable person, I could manage very well on my own. I could handle myself as a single person at a dinner party or fly three kids halfway round the world alone. But I didn't like it, and often wondered: *Is this what a marriage looks like?* Every day I became a little bit more fed up with my circumstances but I didn't know how to change them. Raymond worked all the hours of the day and night and we benefited financially. In the end, I had to accept that I could not change the marriage. All I could do was leave.

Joe once asked me: 'Do you think you would have left Dad if it hadn't been for the accident?'

That is the million dollar question. And honestly, I don't know the answer. In the sea I had experienced a moment of complete clarity, a unique opportunity to look at my life and ask: *Do I want to carry on this way?*

But does it really take nearly dying to change your life? Should it?

Maybe for me, it did. The accident was certainly a catalyst for change. Whether that change would have happened anyway is impossible for me to say. All I know is that if I hadn't had that jolt, that moment of insight, I would never have gained this perspective on life. And for that, I will always be grateful. Every day I get to look at my kids and my grandkids, I know I would never have seen any of it if I wasn't rescued at sea. If it wasn't for the amazing sacrifice and seamanship of Captain Sirpreet and his crew. I am only alive today because of them. Whatever is out there, whatever I have to face next, I am utterly grateful to the depths of my being that I get to draw back the curtains every day and see a new dawn.

Life cannot be lived in a constant state of profound, unending happiness. It's impossible. Among the gratitude and contentment there are the usual stresses, strains and annoyances of everyday life. Things still annoy or upset me, but the difference is that whereas before I may have ascribed them time, weight and significance, today the little things don't bother me so much. I have a different attitude now. I can shrug off a lot of the petty annoyances. I think about what really matters and the small stuff just sort of melts away. The pandemic has helped me in that regard to think about the important things in life. About what really matters and what I value most. The relative hierarchy of life's problems become a little easier to order.

One of my all-time heroines, Tracy Edwards, was the first woman to skipper an all-female crew for the *Whitbread Round the World Yacht Race*, in 1989. I read her autobiography *Living Every Second* many years earlier. A few months ago I got the opportunity to meet her in person. To me, she was an inspiration, a pioneer in the days when sailing was a very male-dominated sport. In TV interviews from that time, for instance, the male presenters would ask her inane, sexist questions like: 'Are you going to take plenty of waterproof mascara, then?' It was appalling that women were not valued in their own right as sailors, reduced to stereotypes and their accomplishments diminished because of their gender. But Tracy triumphed against all these prejudices and her courage and sense of adventure filled me with awe.

Meeting her at the yacht club — where she came to give a motivational lecture — she admitted that when the Whitbread Race was over, she experienced a nervous breakdown.

'But that wasn't the sort of thing we wrote in books, back in the day,' she smiled wryly. Tracy said part of her recovery was returning to the small town in North Wales where she had grown up and reconnecting with all her old school friends. That, for her, had been a revelation. Many had never left. They had married their school sweethearts, settled down, had children and lived very quiet lives within a five mile radius of where they had grown up.

'The thing was, as we sat in the pub, all chatting and catching up, I realised they had never changed,' she wrote. 'They were happy and I experienced a pang of jealousy that they could be that content within their horizons.'

Tracy said she had always felt like an outsider but this alienation was highlighted strongly when she met up with all those old friends.

'I wondered if I could have saved myself a lot of pain and heartache by being like them... but then the thought of never having done all those things, of not sailing round the world, never seeing an albatross flying overhead miles from land... I just couldn't imagine *not* doing them.'

I found this entirely relatable. I, too, have taken many steps away from the place I was raised. They were *my* steps. I know many people who have found peace and contentment within the parameters of the lives they were brought up in, within the well-trodden paths of their parents and grandparents and who have settled down in the exact same spot. There is nothing wrong with that. I don't think I am any better for having been on my journey, but I had to go on it because I wasn't content where I started. The risks and extreme ups and downs led me down paths I would never otherwise have taken. We moved to Hong Kong due to financial woes. The accident caused me to fully wake up and see my life for what it was but also for what it could be. The greatest freedom I had was the freedom of choice, regardless of how it would play out.

It took a long time for me to write this book – thirteen years to be exact. Life moves on and the only thing we know for certain is that change is constant. We grow, we learn and it's impossible to say at what point the story is worth the telling.

It took me ten years to even feel ready to tell this story and another three years to find the time. I left my job and started training for a new career as a life coach. This prompted a period of reflection and personal growth that allowed me to fully understand and make sense of how my life evolved after the accident. Mum died and I suppose that made my story easier to tell. As the pandemic held us all locked down at home for long periods, it provided an opportunity to get writing.

Reflection on life events has not always been comfortable. I told myself stories and interpreted events in ways that fit my own narratives. Sometimes those narratives obscured things I didn't wish to look at or revisit. Going back forced me to take a closer look at things I didn't see well the first time. Nothing exists in isolation and every decision I made impacted others, sometimes in ways which were hard for them. I'm thinking about my children. To what extent I accommodate this consideration is something I am constantly evaluating. A shape-shifting form which is forever focussing and refocussing depending on the circumstances. As Joe said: 'On the yacht we had to work together to save ourselves, on dry land, we all survive in our own way.' We can only really be ourselves.

Life is unpredictable. It is natural to try to rationalise and make sense of it all, ascribe a pattern, a linear path that we can trace and say with certainty – yes, this one thing led to the other and so it was all destined and bound to happen. Yet, the most detailed and well thought-through plans can be scuppered by the strangest and unlikeliest happenings.

It is how we meet these challenges that define us as individuals and allow us to grow and learn. I don't pretend to understand the mysteries of life, but I do feel that I have the help and guidance of forces beyond the corporeal world. I can't explain this — I can only relate my experiences as they happen to me. I keep an open mind and allow for possibilities. A little humility doesn't hurt anyone. Who knows where events will take me in years to come? I can only chart my course, set my sails and hope that the going is fair. I'd like to think that wherever I wash up in the future, I can look back and say with confidence that I have been the captain of my own ship. I was born in Lancashire, but I feel, just like that little plastic doll I used to play with as a small child – I was *made* in Hong Kong.

APPENDIX I

Report to Maersk of the Rescue Mission
By Capt. Sirpreet Singh Kahlon

We take this prestigious opportunity to narrate the details of the Rescue Mission, carried out by the team onboard *Maersk Princess*, on 31 Dec 2007; succeeding in the rescue of ALL 7 crewmembers from the sailing yacht — *Purple X*.

Maersk Princess was on a voyage from Kaohsiung, Taiwan to Map Ta Phut, Thailand making good a speed of approx. 14.0 Knots in beaufort force 8 weather with quartering swells approx 5m high. *Maersk Princess* was laden carrying approx 60,000MT of Naphtha for discharge in Map Ta Phut, with an ETA 04 Jan 2008 / PM. On the morning of 31 Dec 2007, just before change of watch, the Chief Officer received a distress message notification on Navtex, broadcasted by Hongkong Radio. This message was categorized as a SAR message and requested evacuation of 7 crewmembers from a Hongkong registered white coloured Sailing Yacht (Name Unknown), who had reportedly de-masted and was taking in water due to the hole created in the hull by the broken mast. The Chief Officer immediately informed the Master of the distress message. *Maersk Princess* was steaming towards Thailand approx 48NM NW of the distress position. The Master immediately ordered course to be altered towards the distress position and engine room was requested to give maximum sea speed for the distress rescue. All crewmembers onboard *Maersk Princess* were mustered and advised of the present situation, while authenticity of the distress message was being verified from Hongkong MRCC (Marine Rescue Coordination Centre).

Maersk Princess tuned all her GMDSS (Global Maritime Distress Safety System) equipment to monitor frequencies & channels broadcasting information about the Yacht in distress. Hongkong MRCC was successfully contacted and the authenticity of the distress was confirmed. MRCC conveyed additional information about the yacht in distress, and advised *Maersk Princess* that a rescue was requested for only 2 crewmembers, supposedly 2 children. MRCC advised that *Maersk Princess* was the First Ship to respond to the distress message. *Maersk Princess* relayed a distress message for the Yacht *Purple X* on VHF Channel 16 (Maritime Distress and Safety Channel), and requested all the vessels in the vicinity to respond and provide any possible assistance. A total of 3 vessels responded to the Mayday relay broadcasted, and information from vessels revealed they were all closer to the distress position, but no one had received the distress message on Navtex. *Maersk Princess* requested all vessels to divert to the scene of the distress and provide assistance for Search And Rescue (SAR).

Maersk Princess assumed duties of the On-Scene Coordinator (OSC), in accordance with the International Aeronautical and Maritime Search and Rescue Manual (IAMSAR). Search patterns were drawn up for 4 ships responding to the distress, in order to start the search and rescue operation to locate the yacht in distress. Fixed wing aircraft Rescue 32 contacted *Maersk Princess* and provided an updated position of the distress yacht, and confirmed visual contact with the yacht. *Maersk Princess* as OSC called off the search for the yacht and proceeded at full speed towards the updated distress position to provide rescue. In the meanwhile, the yacht was contacted on satellite phone by *Maersk Princess* and 1st hand information was collected about the safety of the crewmembers onboard. The yacht *Purple X* advised that they now request a complete evacuation, and the same information was relayed to MRCC Hongkong and to the vessels responding to the distress. An assessment was carried out onboard *Maersk Princess* based on the information provided by the yacht, and a rescue plan was drafted.

Maersk Princess as OSC relieved 2 vessels to proceed on their voyage, and continued to proceed towards the distress scene with another vessel, MV Clipper Lagoon. Since none of the responding vessels had a dedicated rescue boat, *Maersk Princess* announced it will take the responsibility of performing the rescue and evacuation, while Clipper Lagoon was requested to maintain a safe distance from the scene, and stand by for any assistance that may be required.

Maersk Princess sighted the yacht with the help of flares fired from the yacht, and commenced its approach to perform the rescue. The fixed wing rescue aircraft left the scene once *Maersk Princess* maintained visual contact with the yacht. In worsening weather conditions and intermittent rain, the scenario was rapidly changing and amendments were made to the rescue plan. The Rescue plan was relayed to Sailing Yacht *Purple X* and all 7 crewmembers were requested to comply fully with the plan in order to effect a smooth rescue operation in perilous conditions. The Rescue Boat onboard *Maersk Princess* was prepared to rescue the crew members from the Yacht. Rescue Boat was Commanded by the vessel's Chief Officer accompanied by 2 other crew members.

The Rescue boat was lowered in the water, and in the best power of the vessel, the best lee created still resulted in 3m swells making the launch of the rescue boat more treacherous. The boat was however, despite all odds successfully lowered into the water and commenced its approach towards *Purple X*. Maintaining a safe distance from the yacht, as per plan 3 crewmembers from the yacht prepared to jump into the water and swim towards the rescue boat. 1st crewmember was taken into the rescue boat without any injuries. 2nd Crewmember (Skipper of the Yacht) jumped into the water with a lifeline attached to his waist and his yacht. In a constantly changing sea state and wind, *Maersk Princess* was facing enormous difficulty in holding her position and maintaining a sufficient lee to facilitate the rescue. With great difficulty the commander of the rescue boat regained control of the situation and manoeuvred around the 2nd crewmember and eventually pulled him onboard the rescue boat. His lifeline was removed and no injuries were sustained. The 3rd crew member jumped into the water and was also recovered without much difficulty. As per plan, 2 trips were to be made to recover all survivors, but the enormous swells made it virtually impossible to manoeuvre the rescue boat alongside for the rescuers to climb the pilot ladder. The rescue boat commander in his prudent judgement aborted embarkation via pilot ladder and requested hoisting to the boat deck. It was extremely difficult to hook on the rescue boat with crests and troughs of the swell rising and falling to 6m. After many missed attempts and extremely immaculate manoeuvring the rescue boat was hooked on and hoisted at max speed. Despite all efforts to hoist the boat speedily, one last crest of the swell rammed the rescue boat against the shipside with enormous power. Hoisting continued despite this and soon the rescue boat was well clear of the water level. Inertia and momentum developed from the previous impact with shipside, caused another violent impact thereby damaging the rescue boat, and making another launching attempt impossible and unsafe. The Boat Commander reported minor injuries to some of the crew, but reported the skipper of the yacht to be unconscious after impact. It was unclear at that moment whether there was impact to the head or not. Immediate Medical attention was standing by on the boat deck. The Rescue boat was successfully hoisted and secured on the boat deck and all 6 members in the boat were disembarked safely. The unconscious skipper of the yacht regained consciousness soon. The ship's Medical Officer (2nd Officer) provided all the necessary immediate first aid to stabilise the condition of the survivors and treated the injured.

Master of *Maersk Princess* ordered the launching of Line Throwing Apparatus (LTA) over the yacht, in order to pass lifebuoys with long lines. 1st LTA was fired immaculately by the 2nd Officer in 40Kt winds, and 2 lifebuoys with lines were successfully passed onto the yacht. The 4th & 5th crewmembers jumped into the water with their lifebuoys and were pulled towards the shipside near the pilot ladder. Both crewmembers successfully climbed the pilot ladder and boarded the vessel.

Events dramatically took a downhill approach when the last 2 crew members lost their lifebuoys after jumping into the water. Desperate attempts were made by them to hold on to the lifebuoys or the line of the lifebuoy but soon lost grip of both. The merciless seas dragged them close to the shipside, but before the crew onboard *Maersk Princess* could capitalise on the opportunity, the abandoned yacht began drifting very rapidly towards the shipside and the fear of the 2 crew members in the water getting caught between the shipside and the 20T yacht sunk in. After about 7-8 violent impacts of the yacht with the ship side, and amidst the screams from the water, the crew feared the worst since both the survivors were out of sight. Suddenly one of the lines in the water got taut and when the crew looked overside, we saw with relief that the yacht crew were alive and had managed to grab one of the floating lines. Immediate slack was given to the line and they cleared the dangerous zone of the yacht. Finally the yacht cleared the shipside and drifted away, but by now the tired crew of the yacht lost their grip and started drifting away. A total of 4 lifebuoys were around them which could unfortunately not be utilised by them.

Maersk Princess broadcasted a Man Overboard Distress Message and followed the Man Overboard Emergency Response Checklist as per the Vessels Emergency Response Plan. A Man Overboard lifebuoy with smoke marker was deployed in position as *Maersk Princess* Manoeuvred to make a fresh approach for the recovery of the survivors. Amidst the manoeuvre vessel lost sight of the survivors. An approach was made towards the estimated position of the survivors in an attempt to locate them visually. Lookouts were posted all around the deck including the forecastle. Mercifully both survivors were spotted by one of the lookouts forward. In an extremely heavy and confused swell, it became even more difficult to estimate the approximate rate and direction of drift of the survivors. A lee was created again and *Maersk Princess* manoeuvred close to the survivors. A 2nd LTA was fired in a feeble attempt to pass a line to the fast drifting survivors. It was quickly noted that the survivors were drifting away from the vessel and moving astern. The Master of *Maersk Princess* in his ultimate test of Manoeuvring, manoeuvred the vessel in an exemplary manner to maintain position close to the survivors and keep them clear from the vessels propellers. Lifebuoys were thrown in the water when the survivors were close to shipside, and again to our misfortune the survivors missed and could not grab any of the lifebuoys. Finally drifted astern of the vessel clear of the propellers, but with engines stopped, *Maersk Princess* lost manoeuvrability and succumbed to the swell and high wind. As a result the survivors drifted away from the vessel for the 2nd time.

Clipper Lagoon requested to commence an approach since at this point it was in a perfect approaching position. *Maersk Princess* kicked on her engines and aborted the 2nd recovery while

THE WATER RABBIT

Clipper Lagoon approached steadily to locate the survivors. *Maersk Princess* manoeuvred for the 3rd time and commenced her approach after Clipper Lagoon reported no visual sighting of the survivors. *Maersk Princess* recalculated the last position of the survivors and estimated a drift position. Approach was made towards the estimated drift position of the survivors and good fortune prevailed as they were sighted for the 3rd time! 4 Lifebuoys were trailed in the water at different locations along the shipside with almost 40m lines in the water. Midship Crane was started and the Personnel Transfer Basket was prepared for lowering to water level. After careful and controlled manoeuvring the final approach was made towards the survivors who were drifting very rapidly past the vessels bow. A 3rd LTA was fired from the forecastle in an attempt to pass a line to the survivors, but in vain.

Finally the survivors passed the bow as the vessel gained headway and came close to the shipside. Both survivors miraculously grabbed onto the lifebuoys and held on tight. The slack on the lines was picked up on deck and they were heaved close to midship, where the personnel transfer basket was lowered into the water. Mustering their last bit of energy after staying in the water for almost 2.5hrs, they pulled themselves inside the basket and were one by one safely recovered onboard.

Immediate medical attention was given to the last 2 survivors for suspected hypothermia, and all 7 crewmembers were provided with warm clothing. The Medical Officer started monitoring the vital signs of the survivors. The skipper of the yacht was injured the most during the impact of the rescue boat with the shipside and had suffered a large laceration on the left leg and complained of excruciating pain. A collar bone fracture was also suspected. The Medical Officer cleaned the laceration and reduced the bleeding from the wound. The wound was then dressed and antibiotics were administered to prevent the risk of infection and reduce the pain. Radio Medical advice was sought for the skipper only, since the condition of other survivors was stable. The vitals of the skipper were causing concern since they were bordering around the critical limits. Amidst the anxiety of the rescue and being alive, the vitals were suspected to be incorrect in assessing the actual state of the skipper. After 1 hour of the rescue, the skipper's vitals were rechecked, and to our relief, had stabilised around normal limits.

All distress messages were cancelled by *Maersk Princess* and MRCC was advised accordingly. Clipper Lagoon was thanked for their support and relieved by *Maersk Princess* to resume its voyage. A harrowing ordeal ended in smiles and marked a phenomenal new beginning for the year 2008. The 1st batch of Indian crew ever to sail on Maersk Ships, performed in an extremely professional and selfless manner along with the entire team of Officers and Engineers onboard, who acted extremely professionally to make such a perilous rescue mission a success. The true role of a sailor was fulfilled with the rescue of ALL 7 crewmembers from a Sailing Yacht in distress, without the loss of any life, and only a few injuries in return.

Appendix II

Report from Simon Boyde on the *Purple X* disaster and resulting changes to the Yacht Club's emergency operating procedures

I remember quite clearly the phone call on the morning of December 31st — a very rude awakening indeed! When I called Hannah afterwards I described it as the world's smallest voice — after all, her complete family was on the boat. She was very afraid and felt very alone. I spent the day liaising with the Club, with the MMRC and Hannah and updating people as and when we heard news back — thus keeping people away from Hannah who was in no mood to talk to people of course. A lot of people were being relayed news about the sinking via myself and Roger. That model — of the Club handling one part of the communications and myself, almost as the yacht's shore control, handling the other part subsequently got written into the Club's standard operating procedures for such emergencies. I should stress here that the Club already had a very well-prepared emergency plan and most of what happened that day in Hong Kong followed that plan — all we managed to do was improve it slightly for subsequent issues.

At the time I had done six crossings of the China Sea between Hong Kong and the Philippines, four as skipper. Based on that, my thought was that *Purple X* was well prepared, although with preparations done later than ideal. However I never thought there could be an issue as of course, as with an Oyster, you had a very solidly built boat.

The experience of dealing with the *Purple X* disaster inspired me to start teaching the radio courses at the Club the following year, and subsequently to upgrade the very out of date course offered via OFTA (as was — now OFCA) to the new Long Range Certificate in 2009. My focus on the course became very much of safety communications at sea and good installations more than the trivial of simply how to press a transmit button or tune in a radio as what happened to *Purple X* gave us all good lessons. All in all 147 people have been through my radio courses and this was inspired entirely by the *Purple X* experience. It was while teaching the OFTA course in 2008, and with the recent trauma of the *Purple X* experience in my mind, that I realised it was (dangerously) out of date and hence the development of the Club's own course and its delivery from 2009 onwards.

Lessons learned from this:
[1] It does not matter how good the boat is, something can always sink it (in *Purple X's* case mast — but it could have been a container below the water etc). So training before departure is key, as is pre-preparation of the boat some time in advance so the crew on board know the boat and the systems on board thoroughly.
[2] Expertise on board is a good call — however it is only a partial substitute for getting all crew on board trained and experienced before going out of sight of land.
[3] It is critical to have an alerting method on board — *Purple X* did not have this and in fact none of us at the Club at the time were aware of DSC and satellite alerting systems which are now covered in depth on the LRC courses taught at the Club and elsewhere. In the case of *Purple X* it is "fortunate" that the satellite system installed worked so successfully (and it did — it woke me up!). It is likely in storm conditions that it would have been unable

THE WATER RABBIT

to maintain a link, however, as that is not what it was designed to do, unlike alerting systems such as DSC HF radio and Inmarsat C.

[4] The captain on the rescuing ship — who I met and got wildly drunk with a few years later — was completely unaware that small craft offshore carried life rafts. I gathered from him that this was now included in advice to ship's captains, and certainly when I did my GMDSS training in Mumbai the instructors there were aware of recent advice that small craft did carry life rafts — it was his understanding prior that they did not.

[5] Radios and satellite systems on board small vessels need to be installed in such a way that they can be powered from the main vessel batteries when other equipment has had to be disabled due to fire risk. This takes the form of both an independent wire and switch system from the main batteries, as well as a standby emergency battery, for the emergency communications equipment. This is recommended by the Club although is not mandatory for its offshore races. The club offers to competing skippers a recommended wiring diagram to enable this redundancy in power supply to emergency radios.

About The Author

Lancashire-born **Carolyn** experienced a dysfunctional childhood with a mentally unstable mother and, craving escape from her unhappy past, at age 21 she met and married Raymond, originally from Hong Kong. Carolyn and Raymond moved their family to Hong Kong in 1994 and Raymond embarked on a career in investment banking as Carolyn met the needs of their three children. As the years passed, the two drifted apart and Carolyn became depressed. She believed the family's new sailing hobby would help heal their relationship, but it ultimately drove them apart. Following a disaster in 2007 when their yacht *Purple X* sank in the South China Sea, Carolyn ended her marriage and started life afresh and became a life coach and in Hong Kong. She will leave Hong Kong in 2022 with her husband Martin and settle in Cornwall.

www.ingramcontent.com/pod-product-compliance
Lightning Source LLC
LaVergne TN
LVHW031610060526
838201LV00065B/4803